5 Marks of a Biblical Church

by C. Matthew McMahon

Copyright Information

Table of Contents

Introduction

Most people in America love sports. Let me ask you a sporting question. *What would disqualify a professional athlete from being a member of a national sports team?* Let's assume they are contracted with a team, and that they must meet certain physical and medical qualifications to play the game. An athlete must be chosen for the team. He cannot come of his own accord. He must prove his ability, try out for the team, be chosen for the team and show his ability for, generally, speaking, quite a few people who both own the team and manage the team. As it turns out, there are also specific medical requirements that apply to disqualification. They include:

Dizziness with Exercise
History of Asthma
High Body Mass Index
Elevated Systolic Blood Pressure
Impaired Vision
Heart Murmur
Musculoskeletal Findings[1]

---

[1] Rifat (1995) J Fam Pract 41:42-50 [PubMed].

In addition to the above, there are "General Participation Recommendations" where they are not allowed to have contact or engage in anything strenuous. Such maladies here are:

> Acute Myocarditis or Pericarditis
> Enlarged Spleen
> Fragile During Infection (*e.g.* Mononucleosis)
> Sickle Cell Disease[2]
> Risk of Sudden Cardiac Death
> Hypertrophic Cardiomyopathy
> Long QT Syndrome
> Suspected or confirmed Coronary Artery Disease
> Exercise-induced ventricular dysrhythmia
> Left ventricular systolic ejection fraction <50%
> No contact or Collision Sports
> Liver Enlargement (below level of ribs)
> Spleen Enlargement (Acute or Chronic)
> Cervical or Atlantoaxial Instability (*e.g.* Down Syndrome, transient upper extremity weakness or quadriplegia)
> Bleeding Disorders (*e.g.* Hemophilia, some forms of von willebrand's syndrome)
> Recent Concussion or post-Concussion findings

There are also "Special Situations" which warrant a temporary or complete dismissal:

---

[2] Sickle Cell Trait exertional sickling may occur with dehydration, heat with increased sudden death risk. Harmon (2012) Br J Sports Med 46(5): 325-30 [PubMed].

Congenital Heart Disease
Single Eye or Best corrected vision worse than 50/20
Poorly controlled Seizure disorder
Poorly controlled Insulin Dependent Diabetes Mellitus
Severe Uncontrolled Hypertension
Eating Disorders
Non-compliant with therapy and follow-up or Diminished performance or potential injury due to uncontrolled Eating Disorder
Retinal Detachment[3]

There are also voluntary disqualifications based on certain personal endangerments, such as drug use. Athletes cannot be steroid users, which, generally, disqualify them from having a "natural ability" that grants them playing status. Also, they cannot be felons. Being incarcerated would quickly dismiss them. In current news, there may even be dismissal or probationary implementations due to adverse political views and / or stunts during games, or being part of a political TV program. These types of situations may eventually disqualify an athlete from "being on the team" and they may be dismissed. They will not be chosen for the team, or, will *no longer be part of the team after the*

---

[3] Kurowski (2000) Am Fam Physician 61(9): 2683-90 [PubMed], and Mirabelli (2015) Am Fam Physician 92(5): 371-6 [PubMed].

fact. In most situations like these, their career has *ended,* and in some cases, *it ends before it begins.* Anyone given to watching the professional sports in this way sees that these qualifications, and disqualifications, determine the "playability" of an athlete. A boxer who has a retinal detachment, or a baseball player who is caught overdosing on steroids, or a basketball player who becomes a convicted felon, are all disqualified from playing on the team.

Let me ask you a question as it relates to church. What disqualifies a church from being a church? If a church has a building, a preacher, a pulpit, and people willing to attend, does that make it a church? If a church has a Sunday morning service, a Sunday evening service, and a Wednesday night prayer meeting, does that make it a church? Having a "form of religion" does not mean a church is in fact a church planted by God, set under the blood of Christ, as much as a baseball player who develops terminal cancer though he owns a baseball bat, ball, helmet and cleats, is still part of the team.

So, in terms of ecumenicalism,[4] what unchurches a church? What makes a church not a church after it

---

[4] The ecumenical movement promotes cooperation and better understanding among different religious denominations which is

starts out as a church? And, how can a person absolutely tell whether a church is a biblical church, or, if the church has unchurched itself by its practices, or not? Did you know that this question is not only especially important in today's wayward smorgasbord Christianity, but was very important to the early church, the reformers and the ministers of the 17th century? Tens of thousands of pages of studied Christian literature have been given to this subject of the "ecclesiology"[5] and this question as to, "what makes a biblical church a church of our Lord Jesus Christ?"

One of the most widely circulated and respected works on, "what makes a church *a true church,*" was John Calvin's *The Necessity of Reforming the Church.* Calvin's tract on this issue was exceedingly important in defining what essential actions and qualifications the church must take and have in order to be a biblical church. The value of Calvin's work in this tract is that it succinctly states the principal disputes of the Protestant Reformation over and against the Roman Catholic allegations that the reformers had *departed* from accepted Christian truth. What were the central

---

aimed at universal Christian unity rather than sound doctrine or biblical principles of faith and practice.

[5] The study of the biblical doctrine of the church.

grievances which caused Protestants to demand reform in the church? What issues made it necessary to separate completely from Roman Catholicism? What measures are essential to achieve genuine reformation? Calvin addressed these questions, stating initially, "I wish only to show how just and necessary the causes were which forced us to the changes for which we are blamed." If we were to boil down the two chief ideas that pressed Calvin to write the tract and explain the nature of the church in this way, it would be, first, the manner in which God is worshipped; and, secondly, the source from which we find salvation (in that order). Keep in mind, Calvin's explanation of what makes a church a *true church* surrounds, first, the doctrine of worship to Jesus Christ, and then, second, the manner in which sound doctrine leads people to Christ for salvation, in order that they may worship him rightly. So much of this revolves around worship.[6]

In this tract, Calvin expands what these two principle points mean. He shows how to define the church in three particular ways in which the Christian must be biblically astute. It answers the question, *what*

---

[6] "Let my people go, that they may hold a feast unto me in the wilderness," (Exod. 5:1). Compare Exodus 7:16, 8:20, 10:7 with Hebrews 12:28 and 1 Thess. 1:9.

are the marks of a biblical church? Calvin said that the constitution of a biblical church in explaining his two main maxims of worship and the knowledge of salvation are seen in three expanded points which he clarified as: 1) The true preaching of the word, 2) the right administration of the sacraments, and 3) the faithful exercise of biblical church discipline. Combine these ideas together and one will be able to worship God *rightly.*

Calvin and the other Swiss reformers of the day had been branded as working too quickly for biblical reformation (as if such a thing could be a "bad thing").[7] But Calvin replied in saying that they had not done anything too hastily, or rashly, desiring to show the necessity of their reforms over and against the intolerableness of a *gradual reformation,* which the Roman Catholic Church would never engage in or complete. Theodore Beza, one of Calvin's lifelong friends, says of the work, "I know not if any writing on the subject, more nervous or solid, has been published in our age."[8]

---

[7] See Josiah's true biblical reformation in 2 Kings 22:1ff.
[8] See Theodore Beza's full explanation of this in his *Life of Calvin.*

The matters which Calvin disputed in this tract and further explained were the cloak of evil hiding the head doctrines of the Christian faith, the neglect of the pure worship of God, the sacraments being polluted and administered amiss, and, the government of the church being corrupted by what he called, "insufferable tyranny." This seems, at face value, to be a little more than his first two points, expounded into three points and now we are seeing a summation of a bit more. This is not meant to be confusing. Calvin's desire to reform worship and knowledge of salvation are main theological ideas which have to be *expanded.* They cannot rest simply in "saying" that those two things are important, because those two maxims contain in them a whole host of other theological issues; they contain in them the entire point *of the entire bible.* So, his main thesis gave birth to a well-ordered summary of church marks in three points, and then he needed to explain *why* he thought that the church was marked in this way; this in turn expanded it all to its current form.

The biblical foundations of Christianity are overthrown when these three marks of Christ's truth are neglected, overshadowed or compromised. In being consistent in this, it would do the church well to have,

1) theologians who rightly know the Word in such a way as to stand upon it in the face of any other unorthodox views that attempt to corrupt the true doctrines of the faith, 2) pastors who are well equipped to train and teach these doctrines to the church, and, 3) laymen who are willing to receive such teaching in the face of popular Christianity. Could we add to Calvin's three points these other important points? There seem to be so many biblically annexed ideas to his overall thesis. One considers that if the areas of higher education were theologically sound, and that education transferred both theologically and practically to *pastors* (church leaders) who desire to teach the people of God the Word of God, and the people of God desired to hold to such sound doctrine and practical teaching, the church would be a far different place than it is today as a whole. If Calvin were alive today, he would have to write the same tract again, but with a more pressing angle since the church so easily is swayed by every wind of doctrine, and every level of popular evangelicalism. He would have to write on a myriad of points, I think.

The subtitle of Calvin's work is, "Seriously to Undertake the Task of Restoring the Church," and it is dedicated, "In the Name of All Who Wish Christ to

Reign." Do you, reader, *wish Christ to reign?* It seems like a simple question with a simple answer. But one gets into all kinds of trouble when the practical nature of that question works its way out in the church, or not. Calvin desired to repair the improper worship of God and bring the church back to a pure worship that honors Christ, the Head of the church.[9] Calvin was not willing to simply, "undertake," reformation, but, "seriously to undertake the task," of restoring the biblical Gospel to the worship and life of the church. Isn't Jesus worth a *serious* consideration of the truth worked out in the life of the church by godly pastors and Christians? The Scriptural rule of worship should be followed as accurately as it is stated and exemplified in the Word of God, and this should give way to the knowledge of God. This rule, or principle, distinguishes between pure worship that is of universal application by God's command, and human folly that changes worship into "will-worship,"[10] or the worship of "the self"[11] instead of God. "We should," as Calvin says, "strictly enjoin what he wishes us to do," as well as, "at once," reject every

---

[9] Eph. 1:22, 5:23; Col. 1:18.

[10] "Which things have indeed a show of wisdom in will worship, and humility, and neglecting of the body; not in any honour to the satisfying of the flesh," (Col. 2:23).

[11] "For men shall be lovers of their own selves," (2 Tim. 3:2).

human invention that does not line up with the Word of God. This is important because without a true knowledge of worship, one does not have true knowledge of salvation, and they may be attending a "church" that has *neither* of these. Biblically speaking, if it walks, talks, acts and quacks like a duck, it may *not* be a duck until it is dissected and internally studied. This leaves people in the dark without even knowing it. Calvin pressed the immediate need for reformation in worship and doctrine that did not strictly adhere to the commandment of Christ in the Word. But he did not stop there. In adhering to the regulative principles found throughout the Word of God, these principles not only regulate the worship of the church, but also extend or are annexed to, "all the actions of our lives."[12] This meant that the church was only one sphere in which reform should take place. Reformation would have to affect every area of the Christian life.[13] It will affect the church, the home, society, places of employment, in a word – everywhere.[14] The practical outworking of following

---

[12] "I beseech you therefore, brethren, by the mercies of God, that ye present your bodies a living sacrifice, holy, acceptable unto God, which is your reasonable service," (Rom. 12:1).

[13] "For ye are bought with a price: therefore glorify God in your body, and in your spirit, which are God's," (1 Cor. 6:20).

[14] "And every man that striveth for the mastery is temperate in all things," (1 Cor. 9:25). "In all things showing thyself a pattern of good

these principles are extensions in a right ordering of life in general after the Word of God.[15] But this cannot happen without having a true church that exemplifies itself as being vitally connected to Jesus Christ for its life and practice.[16] This means not all churches that claim the banner of Christ are actually churches, and not all churches hold to the same biblical principles that transform and renew the Christian mind to the mind of Christ.[17] Calvin's reformed church was opposed to the Roman Catholic institution of the day because he believed, and rightly, that they corrupted both worship and knowledge of salvation. This opposition is especially true today. With the sea of religious information we have, one would think we would have more sound biblical churches. This though, for a number of compromising reasons, is not the case.

To go back to the beginning, what *makes* a church a *true* church? What unchurches a church? And

---

works," (Titus 2:7). "...that they may adorn the doctrine of God our Saviour in all things," (Titus 2:10). "...in all things willing to live honestly," (Heb. 13:18).

[15] "Give me understanding, and I shall keep thy law; yea, I shall observe it with my whole heart," (Psa. 119:34). "I have longed for thy salvation, O LORD; and thy law is my delight," (Psa. 119:174).

[16] "Teach me thy way, O LORD; I will walk in thy truth: unite my heart to fear thy name," (Psa. 86:11).

[17] "...which some having put away concerning faith have made shipwreck," (1 Tim. 1:19).

how do we know whether a church is unchurched, or whether it holds the marks which tend to right worship and a knowledge of salvation in Jesus Christ? In other words, how do you, reader, know that the church you attend is *also attended by God*?[18] How do you know your church is a biblical church?

My intention is to give you five uncompromising marks that stem from Scripture, and fold into a cohesive order mimicking the basic tenants of the tract that Calvin wrote hundreds of years ago. There are, in fact, five important marks that are *non-negotiable* without which, a church is benched, permanently, unless they repent.[19] Let's explore what these are and how we can biblically determine them.[20]

---

[18] "He said furthermore unto me, Son of man, seest thou what they do? even the great abominations that the house of Israel committeth here, *that I should go far off from my sanctuary?* but turn thee yet again, and thou shalt see greater abominations," (Ezek. 8:6).

[19] "Remember therefore from whence thou art fallen, and repent, and do the first works; or else I will come unto thee quickly, and will remove thy candlestick out of his place, except thou repent," (Rev. 2:5).

[20] "Whence then cometh wisdom? and where is the place of understanding?" (Job 28:20).

5 Marks of a Biblical Church

"These things I write to you, though I hope to come to you shortly; but if I am delayed, I write so that you may know how you ought to conduct yourself in the house of God, which is the church of the living God, the pillar and ground of the truth," (1 Tim. 3:14-15).

Part of the aim of the letter of 1 Timothy written by Paul to the young pastor Timothy, is to rightly set down the administration of the church. The letter directs Timothy to consider the nature of elders, deacons, and ordination. Much of this revolves around their qualifications, as well as overseeing the church; Paul is teaching Timothy what constitutes a well-ordered church. The letter is not *merely* about setting down specific doctrine, but how the practical workings of those doctrines exercise themselves in the life of Christ's church. In this way, Paul's words in 1 Tim. 3:14-15, are set in the context of the practical outworking of doctrine, and this is especially seen in one's conduct.

There is a particular conduct that ought to be implemented in the house of God. Paul writes, "But if I tarry long, that thou mayest know," (1 Tim. 3:15). The

Greek εἰδῇς (*eidase*) refers to obtaining knowledge of something, understanding, perceiving with an eye towards spiritual perception of a particular truth.[1] In Paul's absence, the church should know, they should *spiritually perceive*, what is to be implemented in the house of God. "How you ought to behave yourself in the house of God." This behavior is necessary. There is a great need for this kind of behavior in God's house. This behavior is the Greek word ἀναστρέφεσθαι which connects the idea of practical living. It is, in essence, how to live well; to conduct one's self, or behave one's self in God's house. It is the way one lives before God and others. People demonstrate quite a lot about themselves in the way they walk, talk, and act *in the house of God.*

The place where this specialized behavior is to take place and be exercised is the, "house of the living God." First make note that this place is *God's house* – for God alone determines the way in which sinners should walk back and forth and turn here and there in his house. This is what, "behave or conduct yourself," or *live*, means in its practical context. Paul calls it *the house of God*, which is, in fact, the church of the living God. The

---

[1] This is seen in John 3:3, "Except a man be born again, he cannot *see* the kingdom of God."

ones called out of the world, brought together under the supernatural work of the living God who builds a living temple,[2] they in turn mimic the character of the living God. It is a living house made alive by the living God.[3]

A house always stands predicated on whether the foundation is good or bad. This house is built on Christ, it is God's house, built on the everlasting covenant of the Mediator.[4] There is, then, a requirement for those in this house to walk, talk, and act in a certain manner in light of this eternal and everlasting covenant.[5]

This house of God may be described as a house in two ways in Scripture. First, it is compared to a house taken for a dwelling with inhabitants. Peter says that, "judgment must begin in the house of God;" that is, with

---

[2] "...for ye are the temple of the living God," (2 Cor. 6:16). See also 1 Peter 2:5ff.

[3] God is consistently described as the living God. Deut. 5:26; Josh. 3:10; 1 Sam. 17:26, 36; 2 Kings 19:4, 16; Psalm 42:2, 84:2; Isa. 37:4, 17; Jer. 10:10, 23:36; Dan. 6:20, 26; Hos. 1:10; Matt. 16:16, 26:63; John 6:69; Acts 14:15; Rom. 9:26; 2 Cor. 3:3, 6:16; 1 Tim. 3:15, 4:10, 6:17; Heb. 3:12, 9:14, 10:31, 12:22; Rev. 7:2.

[4] "And are built upon the foundation of the apostles and prophets, Jesus Christ himself being the chief corner stone," (Eph. 2:20). "For he looked for a city which hath foundations, whose builder and maker is God," (Heb. 11:10).

[5] "Now the God of peace, that brought again from the dead our Lord Jesus, that great shepherd of the sheep, through the blood of the everlasting covenant, make you perfect in every good work to do his will, working in you that which is well pleasing in his sight, through Jesus Christ; to whom be glory for ever and ever. Amen," (Heb. 13:20-21).

the godly, with the righteous, (1 Pet. 4:17). And the writer to the Hebrews, calls the church Christ's, "own house," and says of the rest of the faithful, "whose house we are." So, the church and every member in it, is called the house of God, because Christ dwells in their hearts by faith, as a householder in his house, (Eph. 3:17).

Second, this house is also a special building which God, "dwells in," consisting of a foundation, walls, and roof, built on something strong which gives support to those who live in the house. St. Peter terms it the faithful, "lively stones built up a spiritual house; and Christ, the corner stone," (1 Pet. 2:5-6). Paul calls them "God's building;" himself and other ministers, "God's builders;" and Christ, "the foundation:" for, he says, "other foundations can no man lay, than that is laid, which is Jesus Christ," (1 Cor. 3:9-11). He tells the Ephesians that they are "built upon the foundation of the Apostles and prophets, Christ himself being the chief corner stone," (Eph. 2:20). The safety of the house is determined on the strength of its own foundation, which gives support to it, and *only* to it. There is no other foundation than Jesus Christ.[6]

---

[6] "For thou shalt worship no other god: for the LORD, whose name is Jealous, is a jealous God," (Exod. 34:14). "Neither is there salvation in any other: for there is none other name under heaven

Salvation and freedom from eternal and utter ruin in hell belongs only to the church, the house of the living God, built firmly on the Rock Jesus Christ. Against this house, "the gates of hell cannot prevail against it," (Matt. 16:18).

By *the house of God* it also refers to Christ's charge about and over all its matters, and, all the people of God, which is the congregation of people that our Lord has chosen and gathered to himself in every age. Jacob worshipped at the house of God, the *bayith Elohim,* "And he was afraid and said, "How awesome is this place! This is none other than the house of God, and this is the gate of heaven!"" (Gen. 28:17). Wherever God is, there is the spiritual house being built up. Jesus Christ himself is the gate of heaven,[7] he is the one which gives life to the church of the living God.

This church belongs to the living God, "Which is the church of the living God, the pillar and ground of the truth." The ones called out of the world, attend the

given among men, whereby we must be saved," (Acts 4:12). "Therefore thus saith the Lord GOD, Behold, I lay in Zion for a foundation a stone, a tried stone, a precious corner stone, a sure foundation: he that believeth shall not make haste," (Isa. 28:16).

[7] Christ distinguishes himself as Jacob's ladder and the gate to heaven. "And he saith unto him, Verily, verily, I say unto you, Hereafter ye shall see heaven open, and the angels of God ascending and descending upon the Son of man," (John 1:51).

church of the *living* God. This living God is the one who is active and working, full of life. God is a living God.[8]

In accommodating language, God is described as speaking,[9] seeing,[10] hearing,[11] resting,[12] and breathing,[13] among many other anthropomorphic traits. God said,[14] God did,[15] God worked,[16] God sees,[17] God loves,[18] God hates,[19] God helps,[20] God provides.[21] God is *alive.* "Also

---

[8] God gives life. Neh. 9:6; John 1:3-4; 1 Tim. 6:13.

[9] "...and that thou mayest be an holy people unto the LORD thy God, as he hath spoken." (Deut. 26:19).

[10] "And she called the name of the LORD that spake unto her, Thou God seest me: for she said, Have I also here looked after him that seeth me?" (Gen. 16:13).

[11] "For the LORD heareth the poor, and despiseth not his prisoners," (Psa. 69:33).

[12] "And God blessed the seventh day, and sanctified it: because that in it he had rested from all his work which God created and made," (Gen. 2:3).

[13] "And the LORD God formed man of the dust of the ground, and breathed into his nostrils the breath of life; and man became a living soul," (Gen. 2:7).

[14] Num. 24:13; 1 Sam. 2:30; 1 Kings 22:14; Isa. 3:16; Jer. 9:13, 45:4; Ezek. 13:6-7, 36:23; Amos 5:16; Mic. 6:1.

[15] "Unto Adam also and to his wife did the LORD God make coats of skins, and clothed them," (Gen. 3:21).

[16] Job 33:29; 1 Cor. 12:6; Phil. 2:13.

[17] Job 26:6, 34:21; Psalm 33:13; 2 Chron. 16:9; Hebrews 4:13.

[18] "...for God loveth a cheerful giver," (2 Cor. 9:7). John 3:16 and 1 John 4:11.

[19] "The LORD trieth the righteous: but the wicked and him that loveth violence his soul hateth," (Psa. 11:5). Romans 9:13; Mal. 1:3; Hos. 9:15.

[20] "...thy God helpeth thee," (1 Chron. 12:18).

[21] "Who provideth for the raven his food? when his young ones cry unto God, they wander for lack of meat," (Job. 38:41). "Then came she and worshipped him, saying, Lord, help me," (Matt. 15:25).

we have come to believe and know that You are the Christ, the Son of the *living* God," (John 6:69). This God makes others alive.[22] "For He is not the God of the dead but of the living, for all live to Him," (Luke 20:38). The quality that God possesses in being *life itself* is so majestically powerful, infinitely potent, that he affects the nature of dust and creates Adam through his very breath. Even God's *breathing* is life–giving.[23]

God's covenantal actions in condescension to save people and bring them into his house, rescues them from eternal destruction, hell and damnation.[24] They are those called out of the world to his personal house.[25] "He brought me to the banqueting house, and his banner over me was love," (Song of Songs 2:4). God is eternally active, and specifically active to save people in time

---

[22] "For in him we live, and move, and have our being; as certain also of your own poets have said, For we are also his offspring," (Acts 17:28).

[23] "And the LORD God formed man of the dust of the ground, and breathed into his nostrils the breath of life; and man became a living soul," (Gen. 2:7).

[24] "Who delivered us from so great a death, and doth deliver: in whom we trust that he will yet deliver us," (2 Cor. 1:10).

[25] "And we know that all things work together for good to them that love God, to them who are the called according to his purpose." (Rom. 8:28). "...they have escaped the pollutions of the world through the knowledge of the Lord and Saviour Jesus Christ," (2 Peter 2:20).

through Jesus Christ in the *covenant of grace*.[26] In fulfilling all the work God gave him to do, the Anointed Savior stands presently active in intercession for his people,[27] and active in sending the Spirit of Grace for the good of the church.[28] All spiritual benefits of the Covenant of Grace which Christ fulfilled as the only begotten Son of the Father for sinners, comprise all the advantages of what Scripture calls, *the mystery of godliness* (whatever that is), and surrounds an active, living God. "And without controversy great is the mystery of godliness: God was manifest in the flesh, justified in the Spirit, seen of angels, preached unto the Gentiles, believed on in the world, received up into glory," (1 Tim. 3:16). In this mystery of godliness, God manifested himself in the flesh, worked in covenant to be justified in the Spirit, was perceived by the attention of angels, and from his work preached the message of a new and living way in order that he might be believed on

---

[26] "I will make an everlasting covenant with you, even the sure mercies of David," (Isa. 55:3). "Now the God of peace, that brought again from the dead our Lord Jesus, that great shepherd of the sheep, through the blood of the everlasting covenant," (Heb. 13:20).

[27] "Wherefore he is able also to save them to the uttermost that come unto God by him, seeing he ever liveth to make intercession for them," (Heb. 7:25).

[28] "But when the Comforter is come, whom I will send unto you from the Father, even the Spirit of truth, which proceedeth from the Father, he shall testify of me," (John 15:26).

in the word.[29] This Lord and Christ, the Great Exegete of the Father and the bearer of the truth and holiness of God, was received up into glory to continue his exaltation after completing all that the Father had given him to do in the power of the Spirit.

In the mystery of godliness, as part of its full description towards what Christ accomplished, we find the church described as the pillar and ground of the truth. What does it mean that the church is a pillar and ground of the truth? The church is the pillar of truth, not because it holds up the truth, but because it holds *forth* the truth. Paul's metaphor here is taken, not from pillars that are supporters of houses, but from such pillars as anciently were accustomed to be fixed in marketplaces, and other places of public meetings, on which they hung their laws that they might be public to the view and notice of all men. The church is to hold forth the truth *in plain view.* John Owen said, "This is where the truth of the gospel is to be firmly seated, founded, fixed, established, and then lifted up in the ways of Christ's appointment, to be seen, discerned, and known by

___

[29] "Let not your heart be troubled: ye believe in God, believe also in me," (John 14:1).

others."[30] For all intents and purposes, the church holds forth a cosmic billboard of God's will for all to see in all ages.

What does it mean that the church is the ground of truth? This is where we find the foundation. This is the support. It is a pillar, but it is also a support for the living stones built on it. Peter instructs the church in that,

> "Ye also, as lively stones, are built up a spiritual house, an holy priesthood, to offer up spiritual sacrifices, acceptable to God by Jesus Christ. Wherefore also it is contained in the scripture, Behold, I lay in Sion a chief corner stone, elect, precious: and he that believeth on him shall not be confounded. Unto you therefore which believe he is precious: but unto them which be disobedient, the stone which the builders disallowed, the same is made the head of the corner, and a stone of stumbling, and a rock of offence, even to them which stumble at the word, being disobedient: whereunto also they were appointed," (1 Peter 2:5-8).

Not only do these living stones show forth the truth and publish it abroad into the world by their living testimony as a living stone to the living Christ who is the

---

[30] Owen, John, *The Works of John Owen*, Volume 15, (London: Adams and Co., 1852) 509.

living God, but they also stand on its living and active truth founded on Jesus Christ.

How does this text, then, in 1 Timothy 3 refer to the true church as a *house, pillar* and *foundation* for the truth? A true church is one which is the support, defender, and herald of God's Word. The word needs to be protected by the church. "Beloved, when I gave all diligence to write unto you of the common salvation, it was needful for me to write unto you, and exhort you that ye should earnestly contend for the faith which was once delivered unto the saints," (Jude 1:3). A true church upholds and publishes the truth, which in turn, upholds it by the power of the Spirit of grace. "I will delight myself in Your statutes; I will not forget Your word," is the motto of the church, (Psa. 119:16). In contrast, a false church does not uphold the truth of the word of God, and, as it degrades into false teaching and spiritual declension, which is the opposite of truth, it turns into *a synagogue of Satan*, or even may be called an assembly of devils.[31] When professing Christian churches abandon

---

[31] "I know thy works, and tribulation, and poverty, (but thou art rich) and I know the blasphemy of them which say they are Jews, and are not, but are the synagogue of Satan," (Rev. 2:9). "Behold, I will make them of the synagogue of Satan, which say they are Jews, and are not, but do lie; behold, I will make them to come and worship before thy feet, and to know that I have loved thee," (Rev. 3:9).

the truth, they become *devilish* regardless of their spoken or acted intentions.

Paul instructs Timothy that the church of the living God looks and acts a certain way, which in turn follows the life that God gives it and instills into it.[32] Religion, true religion, is the life of God active in the soul. When many souls come together, the light that shines from them shines brighter, and it becomes a beacon that attracts the weary travelers who pass by and see what is occurring in this house of the living God.

There are certain characteristics of those who abide in the house of God, the gate of heaven, those called out by the living God, and demonstrate to the world that they are the pillar and the ground of the truth. These must be further explained.

There is a vital connection between verses 15 and 16 in 1 Timothy 3. The church is the primary conduit to support, preserve, publish, preach, and disseminate the doctrine of the gospel in the world, "To preach the acceptable year of the Lord," (Luke 4:19).[33] This "preaching" or "heralding" is primarily taken up with

---

[32] "But now we are delivered from the law, that being dead wherein we were held; that we should serve in newness of spirit, and not in the oldness of the letter," (Rom. 7:6). (*cf.* Romans 6:4).
[33] Luke 9:2; Matthew 10:7; Mark 16:15; Romans 10:8, 15; Gal. 1:8-9.

those doctrines concerning the person and offices of the Messiah, Jesus Christ, God's only begotten Son.[34] His work in the eternal covenant is held forth by these pilgrims in this world, and they in turn stand on his Gospel and in his covenant.

Paul connects the *pillar of truth* to the next verse in explaining *the mystery of godliness*. Christ is the central point of the covenant of God, the condescension of God, in the mystery of godliness, incarnate, and manifested, empowered in his work in the Spirit, witnessed to, preached, observed by messengers, believed on and enthroned in glory. Ministers would do well to learn the content of this mystery of godliness since it is the heart of the Gospel and good news.

The church, then, is *required* to be the pillar and ground of this truth – the truth of the whole body of doctrine summarized in the incarnation,[35] work,[36] and exaltation of the Christ.[37] It is to preserve this truth

---

[34] "But we preach Christ crucified, unto the Jews a stumbling block, and unto the Greeks foolishness," (1 Cor. 1:23). "For we preach not ourselves, but Christ Jesus the Lord;" (2 Cor. 4:5).

[35] "...that Jesus Christ is come in the flesh," (2 John 1:7).

[36] "But Jesus answered them, My Father worketh hitherto, and I work," (John 5:17).

[37] "Wherefore God also hath highly exalted him, and given him a name which is above every name," (Phil. 2:9).

among the members of the church[38] and to proclaim it among the nations.[39]

Such a truth is committed to the angels of the church,[40] the messengers,[41] against false teachers,[42] and teachings.[43] The mystical body of the church, in Christ, by the word, is fit for work in the market place of the world. It publishes such truth on the pillars of the church. It stands on it as its support. It glories in Christ who delivers this truth to them, who is alive,[44] and who enlivens them.[45] This pillar and ground of the truth which upholds the doctrine of the mystery of godliness in Christ is the central instrument that the Lord has appointed for the preservation of the truth of the gospel

---

[38] "I will declare thy name unto my brethren: in the midst of the congregation will I praise thee," (Psa. 22:22).

[39] "I will praise thee, O Lord, among the people: I will sing unto thee among the nations," (Psa. 57:9).

[40] Rev. 2:1, 8, 12, 18, 3:1, 7, 14.

[41] "For the priest's lips should keep knowledge, and they should seek the law at his mouth: for he is the messenger of the LORD of hosts," (Mal. 2:7).

[42] "But there were false prophets also among the people, even as there shall be false teachers among you, who privily shall bring in damnable heresies, even denying the Lord that bought them, and bring upon themselves swift destruction," (2 Peter 2:1).

[43] "Be not carried about with divers and strange doctrines," (Heb. 13:9). Compare 1 Tim. 4:1.

[44] "I am he that liveth, and was dead; and, behold, I am alive for evermore, Amen; and have the keys of hell and of death," (Rev. 1:18).

[45] "Ye also, as lively stones, are built up a spiritual house, an holy priesthood, to offer up spiritual sacrifices, acceptable to God by Jesus Christ," (1 Peter 2:5).

in the world. The church, then, must have its understanding of the word of God right. One must even *know* how to conduct themselves in this church. John Owen said, "Churches, then, take care that the same truth be preserved entire, as unto the profession of it, in all other churches. Their communion among themselves (whereof afterward) is built upon their common koinonia or profession of the same faith. This, therefore, is their duty, and was always their practice, to look after, that it was preserved entire; for a change in the faith of any of them they knew would be the dissolution of their communion."[46] In other words, change the truth and the church no longer exists even though a church may have lots of people, and lots of church programs. In this way, as the pillar and ground of the truth, Christians are to know *how* to conduct themselves in the house of God, and know *what* the truth is to preserve and propagate God's will in Christ.[47]

The biblical *house of God* is the place where the truth of Christ hangs in full view. In this way, it is the duty of every Christian church to be the pillar and ground of the truth. This is simple enough, but this truth

---

[46] Owen, John, *The Works of John Owen*, Volume 15, 307.
[47] "In every thing give thanks: for this is the will of God in Christ Jesus concerning you," (1 Thess. 5:18).

is battered and attacked on every side by the devil,[48] by the world, and by unwise leaders in the church who lead it astray. Change the truth, have a *form* of religion while denying it power,[49] is one of the most widely set problems in the church throughout the last 200 years.

The truth is read,[50] proclaimed,[51] taught and believed in the church of the living God. Christians throughout biblical and church history have believed and taught certain uncompromising truths that depict the Christian church as the place where God has hung his truth for all to see.[52] If these truths are abandoned it is no longer God's house.[53] The church is to be the

---

[48] "Put on the whole armour of God, that ye may be able to stand against the wiles of the devil," (Eph. 6:11). See also Matthew 16:18; 1 Peter 5:8; 1 Tim. 3:7; 2 Tim. 2:26; James 4:7; Rev. 20:10.

[49] "Having a form of godliness, but denying the power thereof: from such turn away," (2 Tim. 3:5).

[50] . The Word of God is to be read publicly, (Deut. 31:11–13; Josh. 8:33–35; 2 Kings 23:2; 2 Chron. 17:7–9; Neh. 8:1–8, 13, 18; Jer. 36:6; Acts 13:15, 27; Col. 4:16; 1 Thess. 5:27). It is to be expounded so that it is understood (Neh. 8:8), as was the example of Jesus (Luke 4:16–27; 24:27, 45). Christians are to search the Bible to mine out its truth (Acts 17:11, John 5:39; 7:52). It is to be studied (2 Tim. 2:15). It is to be our delight (Psa. 112:1; 119:116, 147; Jer. 15:16; Rom. 7:22). It is to be all consuming (Job 23:12; Psa. 63:6; 119:97). It is to be memorized (Deut. 6:6; Psa. 40:8; 119:11; Luke 2:19, 51; Col. 3:16).

[51] Col. 1:28; 2 Tim. 4:2; Eph. 3:8; Gal. 1:9, 2:2; Mark 16:15.

[52] "To proclaim the acceptable year of the LORD, and the day of vengeance of our God; to comfort all that mourn," (Isa. 61:2).

[53] "My son, walk not thou in the way with them; refrain thy foot from their path," (Prov. 1:15). "Because my people hath forgotten me, they have burned incense to vanity, and they have caused them to

"pillar" and "support" of the truth of God. A true church is one which demonstrates the public proclamation of and support to God's Word in full view of all men. It protects the word, and upholds the truth (again, which in turn upholds it). It is not enough to have a building, people, a preacher and a pulpit. The true church of Jesus Christ must have the truth.[54] This truth is the entire body of doctrine once delivered to the saints, preserved by the saints and propagated to the world.[55]

The truth which the church of God preserves and proclaims surrounds something very specific: the mystery of godliness.[56] This mystery is founded on the merits of Jesus Christ for salvation,[57] through faith, to press the convert to holiness. Without truth, there would never be any holiness since the truth of God is

---

stumble in their ways from the ancient paths, to walk in paths, in a way not cast up," (Jer. 18:15).

[54] "Buy the truth, and sell it not; also wisdom, and instruction, and understanding," (Prov. 23:23).

[55] "...that ye should earnestly contend for the faith which was once delivered unto the saints," (Jude 1:3).

[56] "And without controversy great is the mystery of godliness: God was manifest in the flesh, justified in the Spirit, seen of angels, preached unto the Gentiles, believed on in the world, received up into glory," (1 Tim. 3:16).

[57] "Even as David also describeth the blessedness of the man, unto whom God imputeth righteousness without works," (Rom. 4:6). "That being justified by his grace, we should be made heirs according to the hope of eternal life," (Titus 3:7). "but ye are washed, but ye are sanctified, but ye are justified in the name of the Lord Jesus, and by the Spirit of our God," (1 Cor. 6:11).

used by the holy Spirit to direct and move the Christian to walk blamelessly before God.[58] God requires holy worship[59] and holy worshippers,[60] and this is only obtained through this mystery of godliness centering on the One and Only Son of God, Jesus Christ.

Biblical godliness is only discovered by the truths set down in the Gospel which surround the work of the Messiah. It covers the means and methods God uses to save people through Christ's work. Its primary goal is God's glory,[61] and its subordinate or secondary goal is men's salvation.[62] It is a mystery because it houses within it the only manner in which men may be saved through Christ, who is the *incarnate God.* God and man joined together in a special union to complete all the necessary requirements to God's righteousness and justice of saving cursed people in Adam and bringing them into a new and living way through the Second

---

[58] "I am the Almighty God; walk before me, and be thou perfect," (Gen. 17:1).

[59] "God is a Spirit: and they that worship him must worship him in spirit and in truth," (John 4:24).

[60] "...for the Father seeketh such to worship him," (John 4:23).

[61] Psa. 19:1; Isa. 48:11; John 11:4, 40; Acts 7:55; Rom. 3:23, 5:2, 15:7; 1 Cor. 10:31; 2 Cor. 4:6; Phil. 2:11; Rev. 15:8, 21:23.

[62] God alone saves. John 3:3, 6:64-65, 17:9; Rom. 8:28-39; 2 Thess. 2:13; 1 Pet. 1:5.

Adam, Christ.[63] Where the first Adam propelled mankind into death and hell by his apostasy from the truth, and the garden of the living God,[64] the second Adam saves his people from their sins and restores them to a relationship in which they are able to publish and protect the truth of this living God.[65]

It is a very sacred duty, then, to be a Christian in this way.[66] They are entrusted with God's truth.[67] The Christian, as a result of this mystery of godliness, of holiness before God's face, knows, then, how to live or conduct themselves in the church – they protect the truth, and, they publish the truth.[68] Such a one joined to the covenant body must then discern that mystical body of Christ, to that which he belongs.[69] To say then that the Christian knows the church's duty to be the pillar and ground of the truth proclaiming this mystery of

---

[63] "And so it is written, The first man Adam was made a living soul; the last Adam was made a quickening spirit," (1 Cor. 15:45).

[64] "For as in Adam all die..." (1 Cor. 15:22).

[65] "...even so in Christ shall all be made alive," (1 Cor. 15:22).

[66] "With good will doing service, as to the Lord," (Eph. 6:7).

[67] ""For thus the Lord has commanded us, 'I have placed You as a light for the Gentiles, That You should bring salvation to the end of the earth,'"" (Acts 13:47).

[68] "Proclaim good tidings of His salvation from day to day," (Psa. 96:2).

[69] "And when he had come to Jerusalem, he was trying to associate with the disciples; and they were all afraid of him, not believing that he was a disciple," (Acts 9:26). Compare, Acts 2:37, 13:48, 20:28; 2 Tim. 3:3.

godliness, is to know *its marks*. What, then, makes a church, a true biblical church?

There are *five* significant marks that a visible church must have as the pillar and ground of the truth. These marks have been, overall, held by the church through redemptive history.[70] Though Calvin summarized his two maxims into three marks, he began with worship, and spoke heartily about the leaders of the church who govern the people. My intention in this is to make the concepts of Calvin's tract less disjointed and scattered for the modern mind, and more streamlined, by ordering these points in a way contemporary Christians can follow.

---

[70] Keep in mind that the Reformed church has always held to the first three marks, with the last two marks of this treatise as an outworking of the former three.

Mark 1: Biblical Preaching Through Sound Doctrine

The first mark of a biblical church is the true biblical preaching and teaching of the Word in sound doctrine. The church is *the* pillar and foundation of the truth; it is pillar and foundation of the Word of God. Preachers should be preaching and teaching sound doctrine, historically received doctrine, true biblical doctrine. The church preserves and protects the word of God to publish what God has said about Jesus Christ. In this word, God insists on particular graces and particular means by which men are converted and saved.[1] The means of grace hold in them God's prescription for salvation and for increasing in godliness.[2] Such soundness, or not, determines whether God is in fact *in* that preaching and those actions the church exercises, or not. If the church changes the

---

[1] "The time is fulfilled, and the kingdom of God is at hand; repent and believe in the gospel," (Mark 1:15). See also Romans 10:14.

[2] Belief in the Gospel has specific points of doctrine attached to it. "...every spirit that confesses that Jesus Christ has come in the flesh is from God," (1 John 4:2). "...there are some who are disturbing you, and want to distort the gospel of Christ," (Gal. 1:7). "For you recall, brethren, our labor and hardship, how working night and day so as not to be a burden to any of you, we proclaimed to you the gospel of God," (1 Thess. 2:9). "...speak the things which are fitting for sound doctrine," (Titus 2:1).

prescription that God has given, such a change will not heal its maladies or save souls. The church is never given any warrant to formulate new doctrine, but to discover, preserve and propagate God's word.[3] To do otherwise is to render the effectual means of God's gracious provisions inert, because to reject the word is to reject God's prescription for holiness. God is *never* in religious exercises or directives he has not scripturally prescribed.[4]

Christians are to be moved and induced by the testimony of the church to a high and reverent esteem of the holy Scripture.[5] Found in this word is the

---

[3] "Stand by the ways and see and ask for the ancient paths, Where the good way is, and walk in it; And you shall find rest for your souls," (Jer. 6:16).

[4] "Ephraim is joined to idols; Let him alone," (Hosea 4:17). "Ephraim has become a cake not turned." (Hosea 7:8). "Son of man, do you see what they are doing, the great abominations which the house of Israel are committing here, that I should be far from My sanctuary?" (Ezek. 8:6).

[5] "And they read from the book, from the law of God, translating to give the sense so that they understood the reading," (Neh. 8:8). This shows that the public reading and explanation of the Scriptures belong to the pastor's office. To feed the flock, by preaching of the word, according to which he is to teach, convince, reprove, exhort and comfort. 1 Tim. 3:2; 2 Tim. 3:16-17. Titus 1:9. Even to catechize, which is a plain laying down the first principles of the oracles of God, Heb. 5:12; or of the doctrine of Christ, and is a part of preaching.

heavenliness of its content.[6] It is the mystery of godliness, the mystery of the work of Christ. That is why there is no salvation outside the church. The church, then, must see its duty to be the pillar and ground of the truth as of high importance. They are to conform to the truth,[7] preserve that truth[8] and disseminate that truth[9] as its God-glorifying function. The church which holds the truth is the *Gate of Heaven[10]* so to speak, the door opening to eternal life for fallen people.

There is found in the truth of Scripture, the mystery of godliness, the efficacy of the doctrine, the majesty of the style, the consent of all the parts, the scope of the whole (which is to give all glory to God), the clear and plain discovery that it makes of the only way of man's salvation through Jesus Christ – God's Mediator. It holds many incomparable excellencies, and

---

[6] "...in these last days has spoken to us in His Son, whom He appointed heir of all things, through whom also He made the world," (Heb. 1:2).

[7] "And be not conformed to this world: but be ye transformed by the renewing of your mind, that ye may prove what is that good, and acceptable, and perfect, will of God," (Romans 12:2).

[8] "Then said Jesus to those Jews which believed on him, If ye continue in my word, then are ye my disciples indeed," (John 8:31).

[9] "Stand in the gate of the LORD'S house, and proclaim there this word," (Jer. 7:2). "...proclaim and publish the free offerings," (Amos 4:5). "And the gospel must first be published among all nations." (Mark 13:10).

[10] Gen. 28:17.

its entire perfection demonstrates that it is indeed the Word of God.[11] Yet, for Christians, the full persuasion and assurance of its infallible truth, and divine authority, is from the inward work of the Holy Spirit bearing witness by and with the Word in their hearts.[12] They, then, preserve this truth. They buy it and do not sell it. "Buy the truth, and sell it not; also wisdom, and instruction, and understanding," (Prov. 23:23). They publish it for free in the testimony of their life. "I beseech you therefore, brethren, by the mercies of God, that ye present your bodies a living sacrifice, holy, acceptable unto God, which is your reasonable service," (Rom. 12:1). They are prepared for glory *through* it, and prepare others for glory *by* it.[13] The church never substantiates the Scriptures, as the deceptive Anti-Christ believes.[14]

---

[11] "The law of thy mouth is better unto me than thousands of gold and silver," (Psa. 119:72).

[12] "The Spirit itself beareth witness with our spirit, that we are the children of God," (Rom. 8:16).

[13] "Now unto him that is able to keep you from falling, and to present you faultless before the presence of his glory with exceeding joy," (Jude 1:24). "And others save with fear, pulling them out of the fire; hating even the garment spotted by the flesh," (Jude 1:23).

[14] *1647 Westminster Confession of Faith*, 1:4, "The authority of the holy Scripture, for which it ought to be believed and obeyed, dependeth not upon the testimony of any man or church, but wholly upon God (who is truth itself), the Author thereof; and therefore it is to be received, because it is the Word of God.[a] (a. 1 Thess. 2:13; 2 Tim. 3:16; 2 Peter 1:19, 21; 1 John 5:9, 2:5-6). Also, "There is no other Head of the Church but the Lord Jesus Christ:[a] nor can the Pope of Rome, in any sense be head thereof; but is that

The Roman Catholic church, or anyone else for that matter, cannot make the Scriptures true because they *say* it is true. The Word *is* the truth of the living God which is *already* true. It is the living and breathing word.[15] It is to be revered and highly esteemed, to be believed for its sacred marrow and divine harmony, and God requires all to bow before it being his Word, His will, and his full image as the eternal Logos of Christ.[16]

In opposition to forming new doctrine and ideas, or making doctrine more palatable, the church publishes and proclaims the Scriptures and demonstrates the truth of the bible by the manner in which the church conducts itself as those called out of the world and

---

Antichrist, that man of sin and son of perdition, that exalteth himself in the Church against Christ, and all that is called God.[b], (a. Eph. 1:22; Col. 1:18; b. Matt. 23:8-10; 2 Thess. 2:3-4, 8-9; Rev. 13:6.)

[15] "For the word of God is quick, and powerful, and sharper than any two edged sword, piercing even to the dividing asunder of soul and spirit, and of the joints and marrow, and is a discerner of the thoughts and intents of the heart," (Heb. 4:12).

[16] "Let the word of Christ dwell in you richly in all wisdom; teaching and admonishing one another in psalms and hymns and spiritual songs, singing with grace in your hearts to the Lord," (Col. 3:16). Peter van Mastricht said, "The marks of divinity impressed upon Scripture by God, that is, the sublime divinity of the things written, the most accurate harmony of the parts and the whole, and the humble majesty of the writing itself, which breathes divinity in every part." Theoretical-Practical Theology Volume 1, §LXI.

separated by God to service.[17] The house of God, in this way, serves the Lord in full view of the world.[18]

This, then, shows the importance of having elders and ministers who uphold the truth, and who have a breadth of knowledge to deal faithfully with, not only, what many *believe* the bible to say, but what the consensus of history demonstrates as what is *true* as well through exegetical skill.[19] Church is never founded on the idea of, "me and my bible." It is never "whatever I think is what it should be." Rather, it is set in the unfolding revelation which ended in the authenticated canon of the bible and is now given to the church to preserve and propagate in consensus.[20] The church merely sees, spiritually perceives, the truth of the word and they are in turn to preserve it and publish it. They are to be sure that they preach and teach what the bible teaches, and so, they must not only be versed in scripture, but also with the confession of the church at

---

[17] "To the law and to the testimony: if they speak not according to this word, it is because there is no light in them," (Isa. 8:20).

[18] "Serve the LORD with gladness: come before his presence with singing," (Psa. 100:2).

[19] "And I will give you pastors according to mine heart, which shall feed you with knowledge and understanding," (Jer. 3:15).

[20] "And *the word of God increased*, and the number of the disciples multiplied in Jerusalem greatly; and a great company of the priests were obedient to the faith," (Acts 6:7), (italics mine).

large. The "church" is *the body of people* who hold to the truth of God and proclaim that truth in its essentials which demonstrate they are in fact agreeing together in life and doctrine. As the saying goes, "in essentials unity."[21] This does not mean "unity today," but, unity based on the historic confessionalism of the church through the centuries. It is agreement in the essentials of the Christian faith as it has been delivered, and as God has entrusted it to faithful pastors and theologians to teach and preach it with a unified consistency.

How should one conduct themselves before God in this manner of preserving sound doctrine and sound preaching, and publishing and proclaiming this good news of Jesus Christ? Churches that do not do this, or change this, are *not* churches. They turn into something else.[22] They cannot, by definition, be the pillar and ground *of the truth* if they are teaching something other *than* the truth. They cannot be true churches that

---

[21] The following saying has been attributed to both Augustine and Chrysostom, yet, its truth is most essential, "In essentials unity, in non-essentials charity, in all things liberty." Once "heresy" has been historically, confessionally, and scripturally established, there should be no question as to its expulsion from the church. As Obadiah Sedgwick stated, "it should be noted, that to make the erroneous opinions to be heretical, it is necessary (as to the person who holds it) that he be a professed Christian." This means that heresy resides in the church, and must be expelled from the church.
[22] "...but are the synagogue of Satan," (Rev. 2:9).

change the truth of God to suit their own desires or needs.[23] Palatable teaching, watered down teaching, changed teaching, changing the bible, is to disqualify that particular church from being a church.[24] Christians

---

[23] The contemporary evangelical church ought to take note on this in their departure from biblical and historical orthodoxy in both faith and practice.

[24] Obadiah Sedgwick, in a sermon given to Parliament in the 17th century, made a list of present heresies that were plaguing the church in his own day. The pastors, divines, and scholars of the day believed these points to be of the utmost danger to the church, and blatantly heretical. They are as follows (this is *their* list):

> 1) The Scriptures of the Old and New Testament do not bind us Christians, not those of the New Testament either, and further than the Spirit (for the present) reveals unto us that such a place is the Word of God.
> 2) That God never loved one man more than another before the world, and that all the decrees are conditional.
> 3) That there is no original sin.
> 4) That the will of man is still free, even to supernaturals.
> 5) That the saints may fall totally and finally from grace.
> 6) That Christ died alike for all, yea, that his salvific virtue of His death extends to all the reprobates as well as the elect, yea, to the very devils as well as unto men.
> 7) That Jesus Christ came into the world not for satisfaction, but for publication; not to procure for us and to us the love of God, but only to be a glorious Publisher of the Gospel.
> 8) That God is not displeased at all if His children sin.
> 9) That sanctification is a dirty and dungy qualification.
> 10) That the doctrine of repentance is a soul destroying doctrine.
> 11) That fastings and humblings are legal and abominable.
> 12) That the souls of men are not immortal but mortal.
> 13) That there is no heaven to crown the godly and no hell to torment the ungodly.
> 14) That civil magistrate is anti-Christian, and but a usurpation.

are not islands to themselves; they are knit together as those who reside in the one visible church of the living God and they ought to know how to conduct themselves when they are in it, both in life and doctrine. They should know this because they uphold the pillar and ground of the truth in its preservation and publishing. They *know* the Gospel.

Whatever is contrary to the mystery of godliness, or changed from it, is no longer of Christ, but wholly against him.[25] Did not Christ tell us this very maxim? "He that is not with me is against me: and he that gathereth not with me scattereth," (Luke 11:23). This relates immediately and specifically to what the church upholds and teaches about him. This, then, in

---

15) That the whole ministry of the land, as to their present ordination is anti-Christian.

16) That it is as lawful to baptize cats and dogs and horses (which some have done for some of them, if not for all and more) as it is to baptize the infants of believers.

17) That there is not true ministry this day in all the world, nor was since the general apostasy which, they say, began since the death of the last of the Apostles.

18) That there will be no ministry either until some apostles are raised up and sent; and, when those apostles come, then there will be true evangelists also, and pastors, and not until then.

These heresies are what they thought were damnable according to the truth given opposite to them in the Word of God. See my work, *Historical Theology Made Easy.*

[25] "He that is not with me is against me; and he that gathereth not with me scattereth abroad," (Matt. 12:30).

turn filters down through the rest of the marks of the church, or not. To depart from God's truth is to embrace the devil's lies.[26]

So, the first mark of a true church *must* be sound doctrine, and its propagation through biblical preaching and teaching in the church.[27] This is doctrine about God, his character and will, Christ – the Anointed Savior of the everlasting covenant, election, salvation, faith, justification, sanctification, and the like – which are all *essentials*. Next, we will look at the second mark, or, the biblical administration of the sacraments.

---

[26] "Now the Spirit speaketh expressly, that in the latter times some shall depart from the faith, giving heed to seducing spirits, and doctrines of devils," (1 Tim. 4:1).

[27] "But speak thou the things which become sound doctrine," (Titus 2:1). See my work, "The Lord's Voice Cries to the City" for a full presentation of biblical preaching.

Mark 2: Biblical Administration of the Sacraments

We find in Acts 2:42 that the church, "continued steadfastly in the apostles' doctrine and fellowship, and *in breaking of bread*, and in prayers." This steadfast continuance included the sacraments[1] as a means of grace, and throughout the book of Acts we can see this in both the breaking of bread, or the Lord's Supper,[2] and the entrance into the church through baptism as a sacrament.[3] In these we find that baptism is the sacrament of entrance into the church and covenant of grace, and the Lord's Supper as the sacrament of growth. The church continued steadfastly in the doctrine of the

---

[1] William Perkins in his *Golden Chain* said, "A sacrament is that, where Christ and his saving graces, are by certain external rites, signified, exhibited, and sealed to a Christian man. Romans 4:11, "He received the sign of circumcision, as the seal of the righteousness of the faith which he had, when he was uncircumcised." Genesis 17:11, "Thou shall circumcise the fore-skin of your flesh, and it shall be a sign of the covenant between me and thee." God alone is the author of a sacrament, for the sign cannot confirm anything at all, but by the consent and promise of him, at whose hands the benefit promised must be received. Therefore, it is God alone, which appoints signs of grace, in whose power alone it is to bestow grace." Perkins, William, *A Golden Chain: The Order of the Causes of Salvation and Damnation*, Chapter 32, Of the Sacraments.
[2] Acts 2:46; 20:7, 11.
[3] Acts 2:38, 41, 8:12-13, 16, 36, 38, 9:18, 10:47-48, 11:16, 16:15, 33, 18:8, 19:3-5, 22:16.

apostles which in turn pressed them to hold steadfastly to doctrine, fellowship, prayer and the sacraments. Daniel Cawdrey said of this, "That the right administration of the Word and sacraments are the notes of a true church."[4] If this is not kept, it presently levels out the Christian with what a heathen spiritually has from Christ, which is *nothing*. God has appointed these sacraments (by which the mystery of godliness is known visibly) to be an ordinary means of bestowing his effectual grace.[5] If they are used rightly, God has promised that they will be effectual to those partaking in them.[6] If they are used wrongly, they are not promised

---

[4] Cawdrey, Daniel, *A Discourse on Church Discipline and Reformation*, Correcting Mistakes About the Nature of the Church Part 2, Section 3.

[5] *The 1647 Westminster Confession of Faith* 27:1 says, "Sacraments are holy signs and seals of the covenant of grace, immediately instituted by God, to represent Christ and his benefits, and to confirm our interest in him: as also to put a visible difference between those that belong unto the Church and the rest of the world; and solemnly to engage them to the service of God in Christ, according to his Word." (Gen. 17:7, 10; Rom. 4:11; Matt. 28:19; 1 Cor. 10:16, 21, 11:25-26; Gal. 3:27; Gen. 34:14; Exod. 12:48; Rom. 6:3-4, 15:8.

[6] "Whereof I was made a minister, according to the gift of the grace of God given unto me by the effectual working of his power," (Eph. 3:7). Compare Rom. 8:13; Gal. 5:5; Eph. 2:22; 1 Peter 1:22. See also the 1647 Westminster Confession of Faith, 27:3, "The grace which is exhibited in or by the sacraments, rightly used, is not conferred by any power in them; neither doth the efficacy of a sacrament depend upon the piety or intention of him that doth administer it, but upon the work of the Spirit, and the word of institution, which contains, together with a precept authorizing the use thereof, a promise of

to have any effectual sanctifying power in Christ.[7] God never promises to bless anything that he has not instituted in his way.[8] The abuse of God's sacraments are never savingly or sanctifyingly effectual in the church when they are distorted and changed.[9] Christians will never actually enjoy their efficacy if they teach them or use them wrongly. Again, they may have a form of godliness, but they are *emptied* of any power.

What are the remedies to overthrow this abuse and sin within the church? The Word of God must regulate the sacraments, and they are to be administered biblically, and in this the church continues to be the pillar and ground of the truth. This would mean the expulsion of everything not prescribed in the Bible by good and necessary inference or by the direct institution of God – in other words, there are no changes to God's prescribed mystery of godliness. There must be an immediate return to the legitimate mystery of godliness

---

benefit to worthy receivers," (Rom. 2:28-29; 1 Peter 3:21; Matt. 3:11; 1 Cor 12:13; Matt. 26:27-28.

[7] "Having a form of godliness, but denying the power thereof: from such turn away," (2 Tim. 3:5).

[8] "So I gave them up unto their own hearts' lust: and they walked in their own counsels," (Psa. 81:12).

[9] "Who *changed* the truth of God into a lie, and worshipped and served the creature more than the Creator, who is blessed for ever. Amen," (Rom. 1:25).

in Christ, the ground of salvation.[10] Such deceitfulness and disloyalty to the Word of God, and subsequently God himself, cannot ever be tolerated. *God is not in it.* To have the right administration of the sacraments is a mark of a biblical church. Christian practices should always consistently be guided by the principles of the Word of God, to know how to conduct one's self in the house of the living God.

Those who have been converted, qualified by the sanctifying effect of the Spirit, and made alive through the one and only Messiah Jesus Christ, bought with the infinite price of Christ's sacrifice, and underneath the blood of the Redeemer, are sons and daughters of priceless grace. To misuse the sacraments, is to live carelessly before them. Some think that simply because they *have* the means of grace they believe they are sanctified whenever they use or attend them.[11] However, exercise in a given duty does not ensure a sanctifying affect unless the Spirit of God makes it effectual in

---

[10] "Repent; or else I will come unto thee quickly, and will fight against them with the sword of my mouth," (Rev. 2:16).

[11] See Jeremiah 7:1-8 where the people "had" the temple of the Lord, but misused the means and God rejected them, or Jesus in Matthew 21:13 where, "It is written, My house shall be called the house of prayer; but ye have made it a den of thieves."

truth.[12] There should be a proper preparation to them, as well as a proper execution of their use as God intended it.[13] To neglect either renders the means ineffectual and carnal.

A biblical use of the sacraments, either of baptism or the supper, will avoid two extremes often found in many contemporary churches. Either they will empty the sacrament of its power, or they empower the sacrament beyond its intent. On the one hand, making the sacrament "merely" a memorial of some kind is to empty it of its power. Or, to infuse into it some magical properties as a result of instituting it, is to over encumber it and make it something that it is not. When the Lord's Supper, for example, is merely a memorial, it is rendered moot, and ineffectual since it has no Spiritual power or use through faith in the Spirit. Baptism should be, as another example, "the laver of regeneration and of the renewing of the Holy Spirit," (Titus 3:5). Is it or not? Is the Lord's Supper something in which eternal life or death is *found?* Paul says, "For he that eateth and

---

[12] "For this cause also thank we God without ceasing, because, when ye received the word of God which ye heard of us, ye received it not as the word of men, but as it is in truth, the word of God, which effectually worketh also in you that believe," (1 Thess. 2:13).

[13] See Jeremiah Burroughs in his work, "Gospel Worship" which has been updated and modernized by Puritan Publications. He deals extensively with preparation to the sacrament of the Lord's Supper.

drinketh unworthily, eateth and drinketh damnation to himself," (1 Cor. 11:29). There is an active principle of damnation that accompanies the unworthy eating of the sacrament as the Spirit works in it. Christ says, "Whoso eateth my flesh, and drinketh my blood, hath eternal life," (John 5:54). Is not Christ the "*bread* of life?" Does the use of the sacrament, by faith, in the Spirit count for nothing? Or are there eternal consequences attached to *it?* Is there nothing in the sacrament of the Lord's Supper but bread and wine? It is not my intention, here, to give you a full orbed view of the Lord's Supper (or baptism), nor is that the intent of this book. However, to understand the misuse of the sacraments, let us simply use the Lord's Supper as an example, and this, briefly.

The Supper is not a bare sign, merely as a memorial.[14] Christ says that *it is his body*, and Paul says that it is the *communion of Christ's body and blood*, (1 Cor. 10:16), spiritually speaking. There is *more* in the sacramental bread than in common bread, though its nature is not changed. Do you believe this? What has

---

[14] In public reform for the church at large Ulrich Zwingli abolished images in the churches, abolished the mass, reformulated baptism (in his view omitting everything that he thought was not Scripturally warranted), and drew up a *new* theology for the Lord's Supper (which in turn becomes the memorial view held by most anabaptists and Baptists). See my work, "The Reformation Made Easy."

changed in the bread and wine (or the water of baptism) is its *use*. It has a spiritual *attachment* to it that *nourishes the soul*. Henry Smith rightly said, "for as sure as we receive bread, so surely do we receive Christ—not only the benefits of Christ, but Christ himself (although not in a popish manner)."[15] Smith agrees with Calvin,[16] and shows that the Lord's Supper *exhibits* something to us in a sign,[17] and then what is exhibited *becomes* ours. It becomes ours, as Calvin accurately instructs, "by application."[18] This, "makes us feel its efficacy."[19] "For it assures us, first, that whatever Christ did or suffered was done to give us life; and, secondly, that this quickening is eternal; by it we are ceaselessly nourished, sustained, and preserved in life."[20] We are so joined to him, as though we were *one body*. Faithful Christians

---

[15] Smith, Henry, *A Treatise on the Lord's Supper*, The First Part, "What do We Receive?"

[16] See Calvin's *Institutes* 4:17:1.

[17] *The 1647 Westminster Confession of Faith*, section 29:7 says, "Worthy receivers, outwardly partaking of the visible elements in this sacrament, do then also inwardly by faith, *really and indeed*, yet not carnally and corporally, but spiritually, *receive and feed upon Christ crucified, and all benefits of his death*: the body and blood of Christ being then not corporally or carnally in, with, or under the bread and wine; yet as really, but spiritually, present to the faith of believers in that ordinance, as the elements themselves are, to their outward senses, (1 Cor. 10:16 and 11:28).

[18] *Institutes* 4:17:5.

[19] Ibid.

[20] Ibid.

not only marry Christ's *benefits*, but also marry Christ *himself*, and being partakers of him, they are made partakers of all his benefits, which includes benefits both in the Lord's Supper and baptism. The Father gave us his Son,[21] and so the Son gives us himself in these signs, which are spiritually effectual for sanctification through the Spirit. As the bread is a sign of his body, so the giving of the bread is a sign of the giving of his body. You might ask, "How does this *actually* occur?" The answer, as it has been throughout history, is a spiritual *mystery*. When Christians receive the bread and wine, the Son of God comes to them, which fills them with peace, joy and grace. They receive spiritual benefits through faith even though they have only eaten bread and wine because the Spirit who dwells in them makes the sign effectual to their faith. Augustine rightly said, "Believe, and you have eaten."[22] This does not argue that a person literally, "eats and drinks Christ," as the Roman Catholics believe in transubstantiation,[23] which is a lie.

---

[21] "He that spared not his own Son, but delivered him up for us all, how shall he not with him also freely give us all things?" (Rom. 8:32).

[22] Augustine, *Ad Boniface*, epistle 23.

[23] Transubstantiation, is, according to the teachings of the Roman Catholic Church, the change of essence by which the bread and wine offered in the sacrifice of the sacrament of the Eucharist during the Mass, become the body and blood of Jesus Christ. (*The*

Rather, the elements in themselves cultivate a lively faith in true believers.

Consider the Lord's Supper in the crude example of a cell phone. As an illustration, the bread and wine act as a cell phone to Christ. It connects the recipient to Christ and they feed off him by faith (their conversation with him). Christ is *not* the cell phone. But the cell phone is not merely a business card which tells someone something about Christ, or where he can be found. The cell phone *literally* connects the user to the person they are trying to reach. The cell phone is powered by a battery – which we will call *faith*. The business card only tells them what his address is. The cell phone, as a means to connect to Christ, connects them to him without it being "him." Jesus is not the cell phone, as much as Jesus is not the bread and wine. He is merely on the other end of the line. So, to *memorialize* the supper is to *empty* it

---

Canons of the Fourth Lateran Council, 1215, canon 1, where it says, "There is one Universal Church of the faithful, outside of which there is absolutely no salvation. In which there is the same priest and sacrifice, Jesus Christ, whose body and blood are truly contained in the sacrament of the altar under the forms of bread and wine; the bread being changed *(transsubstantiatio)* by divine power into the body, and the wine into the blood, so that to realize the mystery of unity we may receive of Him what He has received of us. And this sacrament no one can effect except the priest who has been duly ordained in accordance with the keys of the Church, which Jesus Christ Himself gave to the Apostles and their successors."

of its power and make it a business card instead of a cell phone. So, in the memorial view of the supper, one depletes the power of the sign of bread and wine to be elements that in fact are *inert*. Contrary to that, in the Roman Catholic view, the elements literally transform into the body and blood of Christ (without changing their nature of looking like bread and wine), which in turn infuse grace into the participant *aside* from their exercise of faith. The elements themselves hold a kind of magic in them. Both emptying the power of the sacrament, and overpowering the sacrament are against Scripture and misuse the Lord's Supper. One *empties* the sacrament of its power, and the other *superstitiously injects a magical power into* the elements themselves as the Catholic priest consecrates the host in a superstitious ritual.

These uses of the sacrament of the Lord's Supper unchurch a church. They reject the right use of the sacrament, and forfeit the blessings that are associated with the living Bread of Life.[24]

This same application is seen in the misuse of baptism. To empty baptism of its power, or to regulate

---

[24] "I am the living bread which came down from heaven: if any man eat of this bread, he shall live for ever: and the bread that I will give is my flesh, which I will give for the life of the world," (John 6:51).

its power in an over encumbered manner, will negate the "right use" of the sacrament. Consider the 1647 Westminster Confession of Faith's definition of baptism in 28:1, "Baptism is a sacrament of the New Testament, ordained by Jesus Christ, not only for the solemn admission of the party baptized into the visible Church, but also to be unto him a sign and seal of the covenant of grace, of his ingrafting into Christ, of regeneration, of remission of sins, and of his giving up unto God, through Jesus Christ, to walk in newness of life: which sacrament is, by Christ's own appointment, to be continued in his Church until the end of the world, (Matt. 28:19-20; 1 Cor. 12:13; Rom. 4:11 with Col. 2:11-12; Rom. 6:3-5; Gal. 3:27; Titus 3:5; Mark 1:4). Interestingly, this definition does not distinguish between those baptized, or their age.[25] It simply records what the sign of baptism is and represents this to all who are baptized. In section 28:6, it continues and says, "by the right use of this ordinance the grace promised is not only offered, but *really exhibited and conferred by the Holy Ghost,* to

---

[25] Section 28:4 says, "Not only those that do actually profess faith in and obedience unto Christ, but also the infants of one or both believing parents are to be baptized, (Mark 16:15-16; Acts 8:37-38; Gen. 17:7, 9 with Gal. 3:9, 14 and Col. 2:11-12 and Acts 2:38-39 and Rom. 4:11-12; Matt. 28:19; Mark 10:13-16; Luke 18:15; 1 Cor. 7:14)." So ask yourself, is denying the sacrament of baptism to infants a misuse of it?

such (whether of age or infants) as that grace belongeth unto, according to the counsel of God's own will, in his appointed time," (John 3:5, 8; Acts 2:38, 41; Gal. 3:27; Eph. 5:25-26; Titus 3:5). Again, quite interestingly, in the "right use" of the sacrament, something more than simply getting wet occurs, while at the same time some less than infused magic occurs. Grace is really exhibited and conferred by the Holy Spirit in the use of the sacrament,[26] which is to be administered once.

If the mark of a biblical church is the right use of the sacraments, then the wrong use of the sacraments will unchurch a church. That church no longer represents the marks of a biblical church. Both baptism and the Lord's Supper must be administered rightly in order for God to attend the grace conferred by faith in the power of the Spirit during their use. Without this, the sacraments are misused and the church no longer represents the church of Jesus Christ faithfully.

---

[26] See *Presumptive Regeneration, or, the Baptismal Regeneration of Elect Infants* by Cornelius Burgess (1589-1665). Burgess treats this issue at great length showing the following, and proved heartily by Scripture: "That which the Scriptures attribute to baptism, as the chief part and as it were the soul of that ordinance is ordinarily communicated to all the elect, when they partake of baptism. But the Scriptures do attribute the confirming of the Holy Spirit to that ordinance as a principal part of it. Therefore it is consonant to the Scriptures that all elect infants baptized, ordinarily receive the Spirit in baptism." (p. 86).

Mark 3: Biblical Administration of Church Discipline

The third mark of a true church is the faithful exercise of church discipline. Again, it is not my intention here to outline for you a whole discourse on church discipline.[1] I will, though, touch on some important points.

In Calvin's day, at the height of the Reformation, the Roman Catholic Church thought the Reformers were, "throwing off the yoke of discipline," so they could do what *they* wanted and teach what *they* wanted. Calvin corrected this in that as the reformers rescued the Gospel out of the darkness of Catholicism, the Roman Church strayed from its course by rejecting the true doctrine and sacraments in the church, as well as true preaching, and would not submit itself under the Gospel. So, the true church continued, and the Roman church left its course abandoning the Bible. In this Calvin taught that *discipline* consists of two parts, the one relating to the clergy, the other to the people. The

---

[1] See *A Discourse on Church Discipline and Reformation* by Daniel Cawdrey (1588-1664) published by Puritan Publications. Also see the *1647 Westminster Confession of Faith* chapter 30, <u>Of Church Censures</u>.

way that the ministry of the clergy exercises the power of the keys,[2] is by preaching and carrying out church discipline.[3] Church discipline is either corrective or preventive. In the case of biblical preaching, it is preventive. It is a hallway which gives the listener direct access to being more godly (provided the truth being preached is the transforming power of the word of God centered on Jesus Christ).

Consider that church discipline is *always* exercised in every teaching and counseling encounter that any person has in the church with their elders. It happens every time the word is read, preached and believed. Discipline in this way is not a negative. Church Discipline is either preventative (like preaching and teaching the truth of God which guards against sin), or disciplinary (when someone sins there is a process that is to be followed biblically).[4] The church must be kept

---

[2] "And I will give unto thee the keys of the kingdom of heaven: and whatsoever thou shalt bind on earth shall be bound in heaven: and whatsoever thou shalt loose on earth shall be loosed in heaven," (Matt. 16:19). See also Daniel Cawdrey's excellent work, *A Vindication of the Keys of the Kingdom of Heaven into the Hands of the Right Owners.*

[3] See J.L. Ainslie, *The Doctrines of Ministerial Order in the Reformed Churches of the 16th and 17th Centuries,* for a full discussion of this.

[4] *cf.* Matthew 18:18 and Titus 3:10.

pure and holy if it is going to preserve and publish the mystery of godliness in Christ.[5]

In explaining 1 Cor. 12:24-25,[6] Daniel Cawdrey says, "We may see the cause of the sad distracted condition of the Church of England at this time. Not walking according to the rules of this text; not observing the orders given here by our Savior. As, 1. neglect of brotherly inspection and admonition. 2. Lack of church discipline."[7] When discipline in the church ceases, like in many of the mega-minded churches and groups, offenses in the church run rampart. R.L. Dabney defines what an *offense* is in the church as it relates to discipline, "an offence, the proper object of discipline, is anything in the faith or practice of a professed believer which is contrary to the word of God; the Confession of Faith, and the Larger and Shorter Catechisms of the

---

[5] See Louis Berkhof's explanation in his *Systematic* Theology under, "The Power of the Church," where he says, "With reference to diseased members of the Church, discipline is first of all medical in that it seeks to effect a cure, but it may become chirurgical, when the well-being of the Church requires the excision of the diseased member."

[6] "For our comely parts have no need: but God hath tempered the body together, having given more abundant honour to that part which lacked: That there should be no schism in the body; but that the members should have the same care one for another," (1 Cor. 12:24).

[7] Cawdrey, Daniel, *A Discourse on Church Discipline and Reformation,* Chapter 5, "Application of Previous Thoughts."

Westminster Assembly...as standard expositions of the teachings of Scripture in relation both to faith and practice. Nothing, therefore, ought to be considered by any judicatory as an offence, or admitted as matter of accusation, which cannot be proved to be such from Scripture, or from the regulations and practice of the church founded on Scripture, and which does not involve those evils which discipline is intended to prevent."[8] These must be kept in check, otherwise, holiness in the body of the church can never be sought, nor ever attained.[9]

When was the last time you heard that a member of your church was being placed under any kind of discipline, or that discipline was being exercised in your church? Did the pastor or elders announce this from the pulpit? Was there any explanation or such as it pertains to the godliness and purity of the body? To neglect discipline, is to neglect the holy means of church purification. It is to neglect one of the marks of a true church.

---

[8] Dabney, R. L., *Discussions of Robert Lewis Dabney Evangelical and Theological,* Volume 2, (Mexico, MO: Crescent Book house, 1897), 316.

[9] "Follow peace with all men, and holiness, without which no man shall see the Lord," (Heb. 12:14).

So far, these three marks were those which not only Scripture sets down, but in which the reformers set down over and against the false church in their day. These three are given names in our Confession in various places, but consider Question 108 in the *1647 Westminster Larger Catechism* which says that in upholding the second commandment, the church is to uphold, "the reading, preaching, and hearing of the word; the administration and receiving of the sacraments; church government and discipline." They also add this little phrase, the, "ministry and maintenance thereof." These marks are to be, "managed according to the pure Word of God." So, from the initial maxim of Calvin's thesis and his exposition of three non-negotiable marks tied both to worship and saving knowledge of God, I place two other logical marks that follow these three essential marks: biblical leadership and biblical worship.

Mark 4: Biblical Leadership

According to Scripture, Christ blesses his church with *under shepherds* for the *ministry and maintenance thereof.* "And I will give you pastors according to mine heart, which shall feed you with knowledge and understanding," (Jer. 3:15). "And he gave some, apostles; and some, prophets; and some, evangelists; and some, pastors and teachers;" (Eph. 4:11). Pastors after God's own heart are a demonstration of Christ's promised mercy to his church. They are commissioned by God,[1] feed the flock, exemplify Christ's wisdom and understanding of the Bible,[2] all which is done by preaching and teaching. Pastors are to be models of Christ having a heart that beats like God's, metaphorically speaking. Christ is the ultimate feeder in that he dies on a cross to bring you into a closer relationship with God.[3] Pastors are resolved to be concerned, zealous, sharp, skilled, and wise in delivering the knowledge of God to the people because they minister Christ crucified[4] to them. Paul said, "I now

---

[1] Isa. 6:1-10.

[2] Jer. 23:4; Acts 20:28; 1 Peter 5:2.

[3] See Ezekiel 34 as God is shown to be the true Shepherd.

[4] "For I determined not to know any thing among you, save Jesus Christ, and him crucified," (1 Cor. 2:2).

rejoice in my sufferings for you, and fill up in my flesh what is lacking in the afflictions of Christ, for the sake of His body, which is the church," (Col. 1:24). He says to the Philippians, "I have you in my heart," (Phil. 1:7). Ministers are zealous for Christ's sheep, and desire to lead them as prescribed by God through Christ in the power of the Spirit.[5] Without the ministry of the mystery of godliness in all its parts, without its preservation, there is no sound doctrine to be published. There is no right administration of the sacraments. There is no exercise of church discipline. There is no truth. There is no metaphorical sign hanging on a pillar that is set down in accordance with the way the church of the living God is to be conducted.

In 1 and 2 Timothy, Paul is *instructing* Timothy, and so in that alone it is a proof of the point. Paul had just finished explaining in the previous verses in 1 Tim. 3 that elders are to be qualified and act in a certain manner, as well as deacons; even as well as their wives! All this surrounds *conduct* in God's house.

---

[5] "For the kingdom of God is not in word, but in power," (1 Cor. 4:20). "And my speech and my preaching was not with enticing words of man's wisdom, but in demonstration of the Spirit and of power," (1 Cor. 2:4).

It is the case in every age that people love to have their itching ears scratched by that which comes from the stage instead of the pulpit.[6] Many churches throughout history have sometimes more or less fallen into the snare of the devil in catering to the world to draw people in instead of understanding what it means to conduct themselves in the house of the living God, the pillar and the ground of the truth. Those church leaders who do not exercise sound doctrine, the right administration of the sacraments, and church discipline when needed, *are not true office bearers*. They are as Jesus said, ravenous wolves who eat up the flock of God.[7] Strong biblical leaders are required to show men their sin and the way of righteousness, as Pastors of the flock of God, and they should be rightfully ordained and separated for the task.

"The minister's life is a life of consecration, without which it has no meaning."[8] The importance of the statement is lost without understanding what a minister actually is. There are certain uncompromising

---

[6] "For the time will come when they will not endure sound doctrine; but after their own lusts shall they heap to themselves teachers, having itching ears," (2 Tim. 4:3).
[7] "Beware of false prophets, which come to you in sheep's clothing, but inwardly they are ravening wolves," (Matt. 7:15).
[8] Vinet, Alexander, *Pastoral Theology*, (Crossville, TN: Puritan Publications, 2017) 46.

marks that attend any "would be" minister of the Gospel. They demonstrate a man's capacity to lead others in the Christian life, having spiritual maturity as one who also continually leads his own family spiritually, and grows and conforms to the image of Jesus Christ day to day. Primarily, we see in 1 Timothy 3 and Titus 1 the marks that show a *mature* man of God.[9] The minister acts in the name of another, that is, of God. He officiates in that office and so he must be *sent*. So, it follows that anyone in the pastoral office has no warrant for relying on divine aid and favor *unless God has sent them*. This also argues that if they are sent by God, then they are in fact qualified, and will uphold what God has sent them to do. They will not change God's word to suit their vocation, or their perceived need for success. They are called by God to work a particular work which they must fulfill as God desires. William Perkins, in his work, *The Calling of the Ministry*[10] sets down the minister's call stemming from two main passages, Job chapters 32-33 with emphasis on 33:23, and in a subsequent work on preaching called, *The Art of Faithful Preaching*, he uses Isaiah's commission from Isaiah 6:1-13. Perkins says that

---

[9] Each of these qualifying traits are, in the Greek, *present tense* in both Timothy and Titus.
[10] This work is republished in modern type by Puritan Publications.

the words in Job contain, "a valuable description of a *true* minister." He shows this by breaking down the passage in five ways: 1. By his titles, (a *messenger*, and an *interpreter*).   2. By his rarity, (one of a thousand). 3. By his office, ("to declare his righteousness"). 4. By God's blessing to his labors, ("Then he will have mercy upon him"). 5. By his commission and authority, (where God will say, "Deliver him, that he go not down into the pit: for I have received a reconciliation"). Strong biblical leaders, then, show their faithfulness to the Lord in sincerely discharging the message which he has honored them to carry. They magnify the Spirit of God, and not themselves, in their preaching of his Word, (which is the exact opposite of most modern evangelical preachers today who want to tell the congregation stories and illustrations about *their* life). In this, there is also an important application to hearers, who should hear the preacher gladly, willingly, reverently and obediently. Such a leader is, "one in a thousand." Put it to theoretical use – and gather up 1000 men and you find one who can, "show a man his sin." Perkins says, "not one of many is a right angel and a true interpreter."

Concerning strong biblical leadership in the church, Isaiah 6:1-13 is a fitting text. It concerns the context and meaning of *Isaiah's* confirmation, (Isa. 6:1-4), and the *confirmation* itself, (Isa. 6:5-13). Perkins shows that the confirmation is divided into three parts. The effect of the vision on the prophet was to cause him to fear. It stunned him and cast him down, (v. 5). 2. The comfort he received which raised him up again, (verses 6-7). And, 3. the renewing of his commission, (verses 8-13). Isaiah was afraid in his meeting with the *theophanic* Christ.[11] Such fear is not limited to just Isaiah. In every passage that men come into contact with God, they *become* fearful.[12] If ministers ever aim to be made instruments of God's glory in saving souls, then at the outset they should set before their eyes not the honor but the danger of their calling. Isaiah pronounces a curse on himself, "Woe is me, for I am undone." Perkins shows that God first humbles and casts down the prophet in

---

[11] It is generally believed that theophanies in the Old Testament demonstrate some form of the Son's appearance interacting with his church before his incarnation (*i.e.* the Angel of the Lord is Jesus Christ before his incarnation). Consider these passages where the Angel of the Lord receives worship, which is only accomplished in reverence to God alone. Gen. 16:7-11; 22:11, 15, 32:24-30; Exod. 3:2; Num. 22:22; Judges 2:1, 4; 5:23; 6:11; 13:3-6, 13; 2 Sam. 24:16; 1 Kings 19:7; 2 Kings 1:3, 15; 19:35; 1 Chr. 21:12, 15, 16, 18, 27, 30; 2 Chr. 32:21; Psalms 34:7; 35:5-6; Isa. 6:1-8, 37:36; Hag. 1:13; Zech. 1:11-12; 3:1, 5, 6; 4:1; 12:8; Mal. 2:7; Matt. 1:20, 24; 2:13, 19; 28:2; Luke 1:11, 18; 2:9; Acts 5:19; 8:26; 12:7, 23.

[12] See Noah, Abraham, Moses, Joshua, Manoah, Elijah, David, Solomon, Peter, Paul and other biblical histories and their narratives.

the sight of God's majesty and his own misery, before he honors him with a commission to preach his Word to his people. Isaiah's confession follows: "Because I am a man of unclean lips." He complains of actual sins before God. Many ministers come into God's presence unsanctified, and in their sins, little concerned about how loosely they live before their people. It is the glory of a church to have its doctrine powerful and effectual for the winning of souls.

Men do not get to hijack the pulpit as is so often the case. Such strong leaders in the church are, as Job 33:23-24 states, "one in a thousand."[13] They should be those who are able not only to teach the truth,[14] but to

------

[13] William Perkins said, "According to the plain and literal sense; among the men of this world, there is not one in a thousand who proves to be a true minister. We should note three things in connection with this statement: the truth of it, the reasons for it, and the application of it. The truth of it is self-evident from the experience of all ages. It is strange, but true, that few men of any sort, especially men of quality, seek the calling of a minister. What is even stranger is how few of those who have the title, "minister," deserve the honorable names of an angel and an interpreter. The truth is too obvious in ordinary experience to need spelling out." Perkins, William, *The Calling of the Ministry*, chapter 2, "The Scarcity of True Ministers."

[14] "If there be a messenger with him, an interpreter, one among a thousand, to shew unto man his uprightness: Then he is gracious unto him, and saith, Deliver him from going down to the pit: I have found a ransom," (Job 33:23-24).

lead men who oppose themselves[15] willingly in the truth of God into the mystery of godliness. They are divinely appointed heralds that preach God's message and will to his people for the good of their souls and the conversion of the nations.

The minister is a messenger *on behalf of the Lord of Hosts*, the *very voice of God himself.* Christ gives his ministers instruction in the deliverance of his message which is entrusted to them for the good of the church. The pulpit is the place where the voice of God is heard. The *clay pot* of the minister is used by the Holy Spirit in such a way as to communicate the rational Biblical message which has been burning in the heart of that preacher day and night all week long in his study. The pulpit is the place where God speaks to his people in a unique manner through the power of the Spirit.[16] The word of God is audibly expressed and expounded by the minister through careful and responsible exegesis to God's chosen people. Out of the mouth of the preacher the word of God is a savor of life and

---

[15] "In meekness instructing those that oppose themselves; if God peradventure will give them repentance to the acknowledging of the truth," (2 Tim. 2:25).

[16] "For our gospel came not unto you in word only, but also in power, and in the Holy Ghost, and in much assurance; as ye know what manner of men we were among you for your sake," (1 Thess. 1:5).

a savor death.[17] When the voice of the preacher is heard, expounding rightly the written word, which is Christ himself, it *is* the true voice of God: for the voice of the Lord cries to the city.[18] Although men speak, yet the word spoken is the word of God himself. Is this something to take lightly? Can the marks of a biblical church ever be fully adhered to or realized in the life of the congregation without biblical leaders preaching God's message and will God's way?

The church must have strong biblical leaders, otherwise, weak leaders will quickly unchurch a church to suit the ebb and flow of the culture and the day. They will remove and replace anything that hinders their agenda, and instead, formalize a church to deny the power of God. The biblical marks of the church in such places will quickly fade away.

---

[17] "To the one we are the aroma of death leading to death, and to the other the aroma of life leading to life. And who is sufficient for these things?" (2 Cor. 2:16).

[18] "The LORD'S voice cries to the city-- Wisdom shall see Your name: "Hear the Rod! Who has appointed it?" (Micah 6:9).

Mark 5: Biblical Worship

Lastly, if all the other marks are present, a particular visible church must have a right divine expression as it relates to their exaltation of the Christ: this occurs in biblical worship. If the first three marks are true, and the church has leaders who are biblically qualified for the office, strong and faithful to the word and to its biblical preaching, then the outcome is to fulfill what God seeks – holy worshippers of truth. John 4:24 records the words of Christ as it pertains to God's desire and will, "God is a Spirit: and they that worship him must worship him in spirit and in truth." That does not mean *in the spirit of men's desire and will.* Paul calls that will-worship in Col. 2:23. No, the Regulative Principle of Worship[1] *must* be upheld. It's why the mystery of godliness is exclusive in this way because it directs Christians to holiness in the light of the living God through Christ, by the power of the Holy Spirit. Holiness toward God is separateness from sin and the world.[2] Churches do this all the time, all over the world

---

[1] God alone determines the manner in which sinners approach him.
[2] "Love not the world, neither the things that are in the world. If any man love the world, the love of the Father is not in him," (1 John 2:15).

in all ages where they exchange the worship that God has instituted for things that they like, or they think will attract people into the church.[3] To change the sacrament of baptism to exclude more than it includes, looking for a visible regenerate church, is to miss the sacrament altogether. It unchurches them to disregard the proper use of the sacrament of baptism. Change the sacrament of the Lord's Supper to use elements not prescribed by God, or merely make it a memorial emptying it of its power and purpose. It unchurches them to disregard the proper use of the sacrament of the Lord's Supper. Change the truth of biblical preaching to be appetizing and palatable to those in the church. It unchurches them to disregard the preservation and publishing of the faith once delivered; this is to be seeker sensitive instead of the pillar and ground of the truth.

Change to divine worship is the epitome of wickedness. It changes what kind of worship the Father specifically seeks.[4] They think that rigid worship pushes people away, and so, the contemporary church thinks it must be *inclusive* not divisive. They want to make

---

[3] Matthew 15:9; Mark 7:7.

[4] Is it not interesting in John 4 that Jesus does not come right out and say to the woman at the well, "You need to be saved," but rather, he focuses in on right worship to the Father, done in the right way.

worship as pleasant to the carnal earthly mind as possible. Jazz bands, parades, interpretive dance, puppet shows, choirs, special music, orchestras, Gospel bands, skits...anything they can do to "persuade people" of the truth of the Gospel, (so they think) is acceptable, yet, this *unchurches them*. Those kinds of worldly compromises never found its way into the worship of the biblical church in the first 1800 years after Christ's ascension. It's a relatively new trend that emerged with the rise of Arminian teaching, and the second great awakening with the big tent "revivals" under the preaching of heretics like Charles Finney.[5] Has the

---

[5] Today's prosperity theology is the counterpart to theology of self-esteem. It grew out of the historical roots made popular in the Americanized charismaticism of faith healing with Kenneth Hagin and Kenneth Copeland. Charles Finney was a staunch proponent of faith healing and this type of idea that "faith always obtains the object." Finney departed from the very essence of sound doctrine with such statements like, "Moral depravity is sin itself, and not the cause of sin," Finney, Charles, *Systematic Theology* (Minneapolis: Bethany, 1976), Page 172. Men are then born righteous and only become sinners as they sin. Finney is really a Pelagian in this way. "One of the sad earmarks of modern evangelism, which includes preaching, personal witnessing, and evangelistic tracts and training books, is a continued attempt to have everything so arranged that if God the Holy Spirit did not come within miles of the event, one would still have something to show for what was done. This mindset comes directly from Charles Finney." (Charles G. Finney, Revival Lectures (Broadview, Il.: Cicero Bible Press, n.d.), Chapter II, "When A Revival Is To Be Expected"; Chapter III, "How to Promote a Revival"; Chapter XIV, "Measures to Promote Revival." From Bickel, B. Light and Heat: The Puritan View of the Pulpit. See also my work, *Historical Theology Made Easy.*

church denigrated to change its status of being the pillar and ground of the church for attraction and numbers? What will attract people? What will make them all happy, as if God cares about that? Knowing that the church is to be the pillar and the ground of truth, it must have true biblical worship that God alone prescribes. Otherwise, as John Wilson said in his work, *The Simplicity of Holy Worship*, "Idolaters in God's worship are temporizing formalists that prefer a little worldly trash set down before the glory of God." Worship must be regulated by God. What does *that* mean?

The Regulative Principle is articulated throughout the entire history of the Christian church; however, it was given its classical and definitive statement in the *Westminster Standards* formulated in the 17th century. It is stated in chapter 21 paragraph 1 in the *1647 Westminster Confession*:

> The light of nature showeth that there is a God, who hath lordship and sovereignty over all, is good, and doth good unto all, and is therefore to be feared, loved, praised, called upon, trusted in, and served, with all the heart, and with all the soul, and with all the might.[1] But the acceptable way of worshiping the true God is instituted by himself, and so limited by his own

revealed will, that he may not be worshiped according to the imaginations and devices of men, or the suggestions of Satan, under any visible representation, or any other way not prescribed in the Holy Scripture.[2]

1. Rom. 1:20; Psa. 19:1-4a; 50:6; 86:8-10; 89:5-7; 95:1-6; 97:6; 104:1-35; 145:9-12; Acts 14:17; Deut. 6:4-5.
2. Deut. 4:15-20; 12:32; Matt. 4:9-10; 15:9; Acts 17:23-25; Exod. 20:4-6; John 4:23-24; Col. 2:18-23.

True worship is that which is commanded by God. False worship, is anything *not commanded.* But churches all over the world act differently in their worship services. Is the Regulative Principle so hard to understand?

The *house of God* should be ordered by God's rules. In this it should be seen as wholly appropriate that God's *people* are to be ordered by *God's* rules. Such worship should show reverence, piety, love, desire, and joy in God, and it should be structured and ordered according to God's word and *his* biblical principles. Worship for the Christian should be an expression of God's heart back to God filtered through the public acts of homage by his congregation. We ought to reflect back to God how wonderful and most blessed he is in *pure and undefiled worship.* But the church today has jettisoned that idea to be more inclusive, and rejects the principle of worship that is replete throughout the Scriptures.[6] Doing this unchurches them.

Worship is never a trite act. It is the *life* of the Christian. It is what the Father is seeking from people all through history on this planet. When the Christian hears God in his word, or from the mouth of the biblical minister, and is pressed to obey him in all things as exemplified in his word, such obedience is for his very *life.* "For it is not a vain thing for you; because it is *your life*," (Deut. 32:47). In this obedience, God has not left his ordinances of worship to the inventions of men (as much as men might think so). God has set down certain specific requirements which are to be followed. It was a hallmark of the Reformation to follow God's prescription for sinners to approach him.[7] This was the pinnacle of Calvin's tract on reforming the church, as well as the heart of his *Institutes of the Christian Religion.* God's will, in this way, has reference to the regulative principle of *life* as well as to the Laws which

---

[6] "This is my beloved Son, in whom I am well pleased; *hear ye him*," (Matthew 17:5). "My sheep *hear* my voice, and I know them, and they follow me," (John 10:27). Does it argue against those who do not follow the Scriptures on biblical worship, or change biblical worship, that they do not hear the Shepherd's voice?

[7] "I delight to do *thy will*, O my God: yea, *thy law* is within my heart," (Psa. 40:8).

God has made known and prescribed to man in order that his walk might be regulated *accordingly*.[8] So, God regulates his worship with the intention of allowing fallen, sinful people to come before him (which is unfathomable) and sanctify his name in a manner that God requires: in holiness.[9]

Divine worship is to be rendered to God alone, (Exod. 20:3; Deut. 5:7; 6:13; Matt. 4:10; Luke 4:8; Acts 10:26; 14:15; Col. 2:18; Rev. 19:10, 22:8). Such worship is both public and private, (Deut. 16:11, 14; Jer. 26:2; Luke 18:10; 24:53). It contains God-ordained ordinances taken from Scripture, for, in the Bible, God has given us, "all things that pertain to life and godliness" (2 Peter 1:3). *All things* pertaining to worship have been given to God's people. They can be known and exercised, and churches must exercise worship rightly. Worship was exemplified in families as *little churches* as with Abraham, (Gen. 12:7-8; 13:4, 18); Jacob, (Gen. 35:2-3); Job, (Job 1:5); the Philippian jailer, (Acts 16:34), *etc.* In such worship God was present as he was *honored,* (Lev. 19:30; Psa. 77:13, 84:4; Isa. 56:7; Heb. 10:25). This God-ordained worship is loved and desired by his people, (Psa. 27:4, 84:1–3, 10; Zech. 8:21). All

---

[8] à Brakel, Wilhelmus, *The Christian's Reasonable Service*, Vol. 1, (Morgan, PA: Soli Deo Gloria Publications, 1993) 113.

[9] Men are required to be holy as God is holy; "because it is written, "Be holy, for I am holy,"" (1 Peter 1:16). (*cf.* Exod. 19:2, 6, 31:14; Eph. 4:24; Heb. 12:14).

the people were to be present in public worship, including men, women, children, servants, and strangers, (Deut. 16:11, 31:11–13; Josh. 8:32–35). As the people were called to worship God, (Psalm 95:1, 6; Isa. 1:12), it centered in the word of God being read, explained and understood (*i.e.* in *preaching*), (Exod. 24:7; Deut. 27:12–26, 31:11–13; Josh. 8:33–35; 2 Kings 23:1–3; Neh. 8:1–8, 13–18; Matt. 21:23; Luke 4:16-17), included hearty prayer,[10] (Matthew 18:19-20; Acts 1:14, 2:42, 12:5-18; 2 Cor. 1:11; Esther 4:16), the singing of Psalms,[11] (1 Chr. 16:9; Psalm 105:2; Eph. 5:19; Col. 3:16; James 5:13; Matt. 26:13; Mark 14:26), with the pronouncement of

---

[10] See the *Directory of Public Worship* on *prayer* which states, "After reading of the word, (and singing of the psalm,) the minister who is to preach, is to endeavour to get his own and his hearers hearts to be rightly affected with their sins, that they, may all mourn in sense thereof before the Lord, and hunger and thirst after the grace of God in Jesus Christ, by proceeding to a more full confession of sin, with shame and holy confusion of face, and to call upon the Lord."

[11] See the *Directory of Public Worship*, "Of Singing of Psalms." They state, "It is the duty of Christians to praise God publicly, by singing of psalms together in the congregation, and also privately in the family. In singing of psalms, the voice is to be tunably and gravely ordered; but the chief care must be to sing with understanding, and with grace in the heart, making melody unto the Lord. That the whole congregation may join herein, every one that can read is to have a psalm book; and all others, not disabled by age or otherwise, are to be exhorted to learn to read. But for the present, where many in the congregation cannot read, it is convenient that the minister, or some other fit person appointed by him and the other ruling officers, do read the psalm, line by line, before the singing thereof." Is the neglect of singing psalms something which unchurches a church?

blessings, (Num. 6:23-27; Psalm 27:4, 84:1–3, 10; Zech. 8:21) (also called the *benediction*).

In contrast to righteous worship, God's people are to abhor false worship, what God refers to as *spiritual adultery*, or playing the harlot with other gods.[12] When churches worship God wrongly, God's people should *hate* this, for God hates it. When worship turns the corner, and the inventions of men are allowed in, worship changes from worship *to spiritual adultery. The Belgic Confession* states, "...we reject all human inventions, and all laws which man would introduce into the worship of God, thereby to bind and compel the conscience in any manner whatever. Therefore, we admit only of that which tends to nourish and preserve concord and unity, and to keep all men in obedience to God."[13] Such spiritual adultery is forbidden and it is a destruction of true worship. "For you have played the harlot against your God," (Hos. 9:1). Christ says that such a rejection of God's will is in fact usurping it with *man's will.* "And in vain they worship me, teaching as doctrines the commandments of men," (Matt. 15:9). The

---

[12] False worship is spiritual adultery. See Jer. 3:2; Ezek. 16:15-16; Hos. 1, and warning is given against idolatry of this kind. Deut. 17:2–5; 2 Chron. 28:23; Neh. 9:27–37; Psa. 78:58–64, 106:34–42; Isa. 1:29–31, 2:6–22, 30:22, 57:3–13, 65:3–7; Jer. 1:15-16, 3:1–11, 5:1–17; Ezek. 7:19, 8:5–18; 9; 14:1–14; Hos. 1:2, 2:2–5, 4:12–19, 5:1–3; Amos 3:14, 4:4-5, 5:5; Mic. 1:1–9, 5:12–14, 6:16; Zeph. 1; Mal. 2:11–13; James 4:4.
[13] *The Belgic Confession*, Article 32.

Apostle Paul calls it *will-worship*, "Which things have indeed a shew of wisdom in will worship," (Col. 2:23), which in turn slowly turns churches into, "the synagogue of Satan," (Rev. 2:9). Carnal men tend to worship by taste, according to their wills, rather than by divine prescription, which tremendously degenerates what they do into spiritual adultery.

Wilhelmus a'Brakel says, "essential to religion is the revelation of God's will as the regulative principle according to which man, as a servant, *must* engage himself. It has not been left to man to determine the manner in which he would serve God, for then he would stand above God. Anyone who engages himself in this way exalts himself above God and displeases the Lord in all his activity." Such people teach their own, "doctrines," (Matt. 15:9).[14] R.L. Dabney rightly says of this principle, that it is connected with the idea of Law, "The word "Law," (תּוֹרָה, νομος) is employed in the Scripture with a certain latitude of meaning, but always carrying the force of meaning contained in the general idea of a *regulative principle*."[15] In other words, "the will

---

[14] à Brakel, Wilhelmus, *The Christian's Reasonable Service*, Volume 1, 4.

[15] Dabney, R. L. *Systematic Theology*, (electronic ed. based on the Banner of Truth 1985 ed., (Simpsonville SC: Christian Classics Foundation, 1996), 434.

of God is our regulative principle.[16] If we are cognizant of this, we have a sufficient rule to live by."[17] The question certainly comes down to whether *we are in fact cognizant of this.* If we are, what are the implications? If we are not, what are the implications of our sin in dishonoring God and not sanctifying his name?

Holding to the *Regulative Principle* is holding to the principles of *biblical reformation* as God has laid them out in his word. John Strickland, a Westminster Divine, said, "Proceed in the work of reformation, as you have worthily begun," not, "mishandling the regulative principle."[18] As the Regulative Principle is mishandled, the worship of the church suffers and degenerates. It ultimately unchurches a church. John Forbes, a Scottish minister, said, "We must not suffer this commandment to be changed or altered, or to perish or decay, but we should hold it in perpetual use in the worship of God."[19] *The 1647 Westminster Confession of Faith* states in

---

[16] "The law is given of God to be a regulative principle for man as far as his inner man and actions are concerned. It declares what is good and evil, and by virtue of its divine authority obligates man to obedience." à Brakel, Vol. 1, 356.

[17] à Brakel, Vol. 1, 120.

[18] Strickland, John, *God with Us and Other Works*, God's Work of Mercy in Zion's Misery, (Coconut Creek: Puritan Publications, 2015), 213.

[19] Forbes, John, *The Christian's Charge Never to Offend God in Worship* (Crossville: Puritan Publications, 2018), 73.

25:4, that the church, "hath been sometimes more, sometimes less visible. And particular churches, which are members thereof, are more or less pure, according as the doctrine of the gospel is taught and embraced, ordinances administered, *and public worship performed more or less purely in them.*" This *practically* means that a church does not necessarily unchurch itself if it holds to the basic foundational doctrines of Scripture, but it can degenerate its honor to Jesus Christ to the point that it cripples itself in worship, spiritual vigor, liveliness, and its commissioned work in the world by additions or subtractions to worship.[20] When this occurs, why would a Christian *want* to remain in such a body? Why would that body want to continue in that way which angers God? George Gillespie comments on this when he says, "the true life of godliness is smothered down and

---

[20] Hear George Gillespie, "Besides all this, there is nothing which any way pertaineth to the worship of God left to the determination of human laws, beside the mere circumstances, which neither have any holiness in them, forasmuch as they have no other use and praise in sacred than they have in civil things, nor yet were particularly determinable in Scripture, because they are infinite; but sacred, significant ceremonies, such as cross, kneeling, surplice, holidays, bishopping, *etc.*, which have no use and praise except in religion only, and which, also, were most easily determinable (yet not determined) within those bounds which God did set to his written word, are such things as God never left to the determination of any human law," Gillespie's *English Popish Ceremonies The Works of George Gillespie*, edited by William M. Hetherington (Edinburgh: Robert Ogle and Oliver and Boyd, 1846) l.xii.

suppressed by the burden of these human inventions."[21] Can a Christian thrive and grow under suppression? Can they flourish under a burden?

John Forbes said, "All things done before God in ordering his church are the commandments of the living God. Otherwise, the Apostle would never have charged Timothy, and in him all pastors in such a manner, as in the sight of God and of Christ Jesus, to keep this commandment without *spot or blemish*,"[22] he said this referring to 1 Timothy 6:13-14[23] and the Regulative Principle. One would think that such "blemishes" are something Reformed Christians do not really need to think about. They are in fact *worshipping God as he requires*, correct? But such is far from the case, for most "reformed" churches today have discarded this Regulative Principle, or they have changed it to their detriment to suit their personal taste in worship.[24]

---

[21] Ibid, 1.viii.

[22] Forbes, 41.

[23] "I give thee charge in the sight of God, who quickeneth all things, and before Christ Jesus, who before Pontius Pilate witnessed a good confession; That thou keep this commandment without spot, unrebukeable, until the appearing of our Lord Jesus Christ," (1 Tim. 6:13-14).

[24] In this, Gillespie says, "By communicating with idolaters in their rites and ceremonies, we ourselves become guilty of idolatry." See his *Dispute Against the English Popish Ceremonies*, (1637), chapter 2, 80.

Forbes says, "We have more need to look to ourselves in this, seeing there is no precept of God which has been more adulterated and violated than this precept of the Apostle. Yes, not only in popery is this so, but this violation remains in the Reformed churches themselves."[25] *The Westminster Larger Catechism* question 110 says that God will enact, "his revengeful indignation against all false worship, as being a spiritual whoredom." This should *scare* most churches. This follows Paul's question on worship when he asks, "...do we provoke the Lord to jealousy?" (1 Cor. 10:22). Or as Jeremiah says, "Do they provoke me to anger?" says the LORD. "Do they not provoke themselves, to the shame of their own faces?" (Jer. 7:19).[26] Practically speaking, it would behoove every Christian to ask themselves if they and their church are "spiritual whores" in light of God's worship. Have they suited and changed the Regulative Principle to their own tastes? In such things, God is very jealous of his name and worship; and in the end, he promises to enact judgment.[27]

When God regulates worship, certain unavoidable conclusions are made from these biblical mandates. If God

---

[25] Forbes, 68.
[26] See also Ezek. 16:26-27; Deut. 32:16-20.
[27] See Leviticus 10:3.

has *prohibited* something in worship, we are not allowed to do it. If God has *commanded* something in worship, we must do it. If God has *not commanded it*, we are not allowed to do it; and in addition, we must discern this even if Scripture is not as explicit as we would like it to be on a particular matter. God, in this way, stands upon the little things in his worship. John Calvin said, "God has been pleased to prescribe in his Law what is lawful and right, and thus astrict men to a certain rule, lest any should allow themselves to devise a worship of their own."[28] In his *Necessity of Reforming the Church*, Calvin says,

"Moreover, the rule which distinguishes between pure and vitiated worship is of universal application, in order that we may not adopt *any device* which seems fit to ourselves, but look to the injunctions of him who alone is entitled to prescribe. Therefore, if we would have him to approve our worship, this rule, which he everywhere enforces with the utmost strictness, must be carefully observed. For there is a twofold reason why the Lord, in condemning and prohibiting all fictitious worship, requires us to give obedience only to his own voice. First, it tends greatly to establish his authority that we do not follow our own pleasure, but depend entirely on his sovereignty; and, secondly, such is our folly, that when we are left at liberty, all we

---

[28] Calvin, John, *Institutes of the Christian Religion*, Vol. 1, (Edinburgh: The Calvin Translation Society), 143.

are able to do is to go astray. And then when once we have turned aside from the right path, there is no end to our wanderings, until we get buried under a multitude of superstitions. Justly, therefore, does the Lord, in order to assert his full right of dominion, strictly enjoin what he wishes us to do, and at once reject all human devices which are at variance with his command. Justly, too, does he, in express terms, define our limits, that we may not, by fabricating perverse modes of worship, provoke his anger against us."[29]

In considering the practical nature of trying to overhaul a church back to Reformed worship, Calvin comments, "I know how difficult it is to persuade the world that God disapproves of all modes of worship not expressly sanctioned by his word."[30] But this never allows the church to continue in its excuses to add in the inventions of men. John Knox echoes Calvin's sentiments when he says, "All worshipping, honoring or service invented by the brain of man in the religion of God, without his own express commandment, is idolatry. The mass is invented by the brain of man without any commandment of God. Therefore, it is

---

[29] See Calvin's complete work online at A Puritan's Mind.
[30] Calvin, John, *On the Necessity of Reforming the Church, Selected Works of John Calvin: Tracts and Letters*. 1.128-129.

idolatry."[31] Knox taught that, "Disobedience to God's voice is not only when man doth wickedly contrary to the precepts of God, but also when of good zeal, or good intent, as we commonly speak, man doeth anything to the honor or service of God not commanded by the express Word of God."[32] He rightly said, "Man may neither make nor devise religion [*i.e.* worship] that is acceptable to God, but he is bound to observe and keep the religion [worship] that he has received from God, without any change."[33] In his work, *A Vindication of the Doctrine that the Sacrifice of the Mass is Idolatry*, Knox says, "We may not think us so free nor wise, that we may do unto God, and unto his honor, what we think expedient."[34] Such inventions and changes unchurch a church.

---

[31]Knox, John, *The Works of John Knox*, Volume 3, (Edinburgh; James Thin, 1845) p. 34.

[32] Knox, John *Works*, Volume 4, p. 37.

[33] Ibid, Volume 1, p. 194. Knox also taught concerning the Lord's Supper, "The Sacraments of the New Testament ought to be administered just as they were instituted by Christ and practiced by the Apostles. Nothing ought to be added to them or diminished from them," (*Works*, 1:194).

[34] See also the *1560 Scots Confession*, "And evil works, we affirm not only those that expressedly are done against God's commandment, but those also that, in matters of religion and worshipping of God, have no other assurance but the invention and opinion of man: which God from the beginning has ever rejected, as by the prophet Isaiah, and by our master Christ Jesus, we are taught in these words: In vain do they worship me, teaching the doctrines and precepts of men." (*cf.* 1 John 3:4; Isa. 29:13; Matt. 15:9; Mark 7:7).

Conclusion

There are five biblical and historical unified marks of the church without which it begins to denigrate into, "the synagogue of Satan."[1] What a terrible and offensive description this is of groups of people "trying to do the right thing in sincerity before God." But this is not about merely being sincere. *The 1647 Westminster Confession of Faith* ties these marks to the *peace of the church*, without which it can have *no* peace. *The Directory of Public Worship* says, "Whereas an happy unity, and uniformity in religion amongst the kirks of Christ, in these three kingdoms, united under one Sovereign, having been long and earnestly wished for by the godly a well-affected amongst us, was propounded as a main article of the large treaty, without which band and bulwark, no safe, well-grounded, and lasting peace could be expected." All this pertains directly to the five marks: sound doctrine, the right administration of the sacraments, the right exercise of church discipline, strong biblical leadership, and true worship that follows the Regulative Principle.

---

[1] Revelation 2:9, 3:9.

How does being the pillar and ground of the truth play out in the life of your church in these ways? What motivates you when you come to church? How do you think about what is to happen in the service or life of the church? The church is changing for the worse in our day. Some today say, "I don't really like the way the church service is laid out." They say, "Your order of worship doesn't really do it for me." Or, "I didn't like when your pastor said that everyone is a sinner and they all hate God until they are converted." Today, people are thinking, "Why can't the pastor's wife be a pastor too?" How many more issues are they swirling about the "church" on social justice, gender roles, political correctness and the like? The atmosphere in the church today is running straight towards being inclusive at the expense of *being the church of Jesus Christ.* The church *must be* the pillar and the ground of the truth. That means that we are not here to set down *what we like,* but since it's *the house of God,* since it's God's ordained means of saving men from death and hell, which includes saving you, that we yield to what God directs in his word, not what we like or desire. It is *his* mystery of godliness in Christ. It is *his* merited work, his will, his way. It is all for him; it is all for Christ, "...that he might fill all things," (Eph. 4:10). It's all about Jesus, and its not all about how many people can be packed into the pews.

One might object, and say "well, is this *really* what *God* wants? Or is it just your opinion?" "Is this how the church is the pillar and ground of the truth to the world?" The answer comes in three ways.

[1] First, Scripturally, yes, the Regulative Principle of the worship, God's principle of church life and worship, is set down in that very easy and succinct biblical manner, *God alone determines the manner in which sinners approach him.* This is in opposition to, "In vain do they worship Me, teaching as doctrines the commandments of men," (Matt. 15:9). There is a right way to present yourself to God *and a wrong way.* You mean not everyone gets a gold star for showing up? Not everyone is a winner? Not everyone's opinion counts as much as another's? No. There is a right way to publish the truth, to stand upon it, to be grounded in it, and *a wrong way.* If there wasn't, then we would *not need a bible.* If everyone's opinion mattered, God's directives would not matter at all. The main text in 1 Timothy which we began with tells us that this all surrounds a very specific teaching on the mystery of godliness where the church is the pillar and ground of the truth. It is all

set directly in the context of how to conduct yourself in the house of God. This is what constitutes practical Christian living and its godly expression in the church.

[2] Second, historically, this is not only what is clearly stated in Scripture, but also what historical confessions biblically teach. *The 1647 Westminster Confession* says in chapter 21, "The light of nature showeth that there is a God, who hath lordship and sovereignty over all; is good, and doeth good unto all; and is therefore to be feared, loved, praised, called upon, trusted in, and served with all the heart, and with all the soul, and with all the might. But the acceptable way of worshipping the true God is instituted by himself, and so limited to his own revealed will, that he may not be worshipped according to the imaginations and devices of men, or the suggestions of Satan, under any visible representations or any other way not prescribed in the Holy Scripture." Many churches have changed church life and worship to suit the world; to be attractive to the world in order to make church more palatable. It is one of the reasons why they have filled sanctuaries and multiple Sunday services. They have so many interested people in what they are offering. But, frighteningly, they are denied the power that accompanies its blessing.

[3] Thirdly, this principle is not only what the historic church believed but it is the very essence of Protestantism. Calvin's *Necessity of Reforming the Church* was a very important document that explained the separation of the Protestants from the Roman Catholics. He wrote it because people were saying, "we don't have vestments, and idols and crucifixes, and images of saints, and incense burning like the mass does, and we don't have processions and high holy days, or more modernized worship," where today we say, "we don't have the mime, and the puppet shows and interpretive dance, the parades and the big band and the choir." Church *is boring without those things*. However, the church is not patterned after the temple as the Roman Catholics have done. The temple was a shadow of the object lessons for the visual eye, a type of what would be fulfilled in Christ. Jesus said, "It is finished," (John 19:30), not *almost* finished, or *somewhat* finished, or *kinda* finished. Cutting and killing and sprinkling, and the mercy seat and the pomp and circumstance of the temple in choirs and special music and instruments and all the worship by proxy that occurred, all pointed to the *fulfillment* of the Messiah who would do away with all that when he finished it all on the cross! Roman

Catholicism tried to revive the Old Testament temple in innumerable ways, and unfortunately, many contemporary churches borrowed their revival of those accoutrements in both theory and practice. Priests and temples and incense and altars and choirs and bands and such are all dead weight to Christ. It is no wonder that the first uninspired hymn in the church was brought in by the heretic *Arius* to propagate the false teaching. And the first use of musical instruments was in the 8th century by Pope Vitalian in the Roman church. Why do contemporary churches follow them?

The church is not patterned after the temple, it is patterned after the *synagogue.* What did they do in the synagogue? Christ fulfilled the temple rites being the High Priest of those called out of the world, and called to the Word of God.[2] He merited, completed and fulfilled all Old Testament types and shadows so that the pure Gospel, the mystery of godliness, could be preserved and published in Spirit and truth, clearly and plainly. Christ tore the veil of the temple down, and yet, so many churches want to go back behind the veil. Why do they want to change God's prescription for truth, for the sacraments, for worship, for leadership, for things

---

[2] See Hebrews in chapters 5-9.

passed away and things that are shadows? They do this because it looks more luxurious, it looks more formal, it looks more exciting and it makes the truth exciting to a worldly heart. You see, the plain truth to many is not exciting. They would rather have a show, some kind of object lesson with their *eyes* that they can either partake in or stand there while others worship for them (which is worship by proxy); but all that is done away with by Christ on the cross. "Let me go *experience* church, because I don't want to rely on having to *know* things." "Discipline – no I don't want that. That doesn't make me *feel* good." "I love Jesus and it's enough for me, don't bother me with any more sound doctrine. All I *need* is Jesus."

Jesus Christ made church easier by doing away with formality, but he also made it more exclusive. He made the pillar and the ground of the truth something accomplished by spiritual believers instead of the pomp and circumstance of the temple's object lessons that Christ fulfilled in his incarnation, death, resurrection and present intercession, *his mystery of godliness*. The simplicity of worship (patterned after the synagogue) can be seen when James says of the church, "For if there should come *into your assembly* a man with gold rings, in fine apparel, and there should also come in a poor man in filthy clothes," (James 2:2),[3] (*i.e. your synagogue*). Do you know what the pillar and the ground of the truth does in demonstrating itself to the world as those called out by God to assemble together as a congregation and proclaim his truth? It does what God has always prescribed. In ancient times the synagogue did this:

> There was an initial blessing / invocation surrounding worship and the attributes of God.
> Next the "psalms" section occurred where they were sung, and also used for prayer.
> Next was the Amidah (meaning standing) where there would be given the 18 blessings, and then a silent prayer was personally encouraged.
> Then came the reading of the Torah, and a prayer.
> Then came the sermon on a text.
> Then finally the blessing.
> In some cases there would be a subsequent Kiddush which was a blessing over the wine in the sabbath hall for a fellowship.

---

[3] ἐὰν γὰρ εἰσέλθη εἰς συναγωγὴν (James 2:2).

Look at the life and worship of the early church. Look at the life and worship of Geneva under Calvin. Look at the life and worship of the Scottish Church under John Knox. Look at the life and worship of England at the time of the Westminster Assembly. The life of the church in its liturgy is all *basically* the same. Do you think your church would attract more people if you had parades and puppet shows and mime and bands and the like? Of course it would attract all sorts of worldly people. But is that what the living God desires of the pillar and the ground of the truth? What a reproach that would bring on Christ to say to him, "I don't recognize your fulfillment Lord, and instead, I want my carnal object lessons, I want the worship by proxy and the bands, I want the singers and the musicians and the praise teams, I want those things that make the temple look attractive because they make *me feel good.*" They are really saying, *I want to change sound doctrine*, not preserve it. That is not the manner in which God has laid out his truth, nor is it the way the mystery of godliness operates. Paul instructed Timothy to conduct himself in a specific manner. The church is to set forth Christ's Gospel in all its simplicity, in spirit and truth, fixed in the market place of the world, in which unbelievers can see why the people of God are different than a rock concert or Hollywood theater. *Spirit and truth* is in sound doctrine, and specifically, *without* the pomp and circumstance of the temple. That was Christ's argument to the Samaritan woman in John 4; the temple is done and all its pomp and circumstance is done. We hang our lives and conduct before each other and the world and God has so set certain principles through Christ which might be public to the view and notice of all men. The church is to hold forth the truth in plain view. That makes Christianity hard in every age of the church because that means Christians have to be *educated*. It means they have to be *contenders for the faith*. They are never to be like Mr. Byends with his silver slippers following every wind or change of doctrine that comes floating by because it suits him and he likes it.[4]

What should we do as the church, as the pillar and ground of the truth? Practically, start with prayer. Pray for the ministers who preach the truth for the glory of Christ, and pray for your church that it remains the pillar and ground of the truth amidst the ecclesiastical temptations to the contrary. You may be excited about all the things going on right now in your church. What

---

[4] See John Bunyan's *Pilgrim's Progress.*

will you feel like in a year? In five years? What will you think about it when growth may be a trickle, and people sneer at you because they don't like God's prescription for the church and the mystery of godliness is too restrictive? Many people today gripe about the size of their church. Success to them is numbers. However, it does not matter if you have 10 or 10,000 in the congregation so long as you have Christ, the truth, and the marks of a biblical church. The church at Corinth was big. The covenanter's churches in Scotland were small. Almost all puritan churches (with a few exceptions) were less than thirty members with giants of the faith like Watson, Owen and others, preaching in them weekly. How do you, then, see, support, and conduct yourself in the pillar and ground of the truth, the house of the living God for the glory of publishing the mystery of godliness in Christ to the world for God's honor, your sanctifying good and the salvation of souls?

Other Worthy Books by Puritan Publications

Seeing Christ Clearly
by C. Matthew McMahon
How did Jesus view himself in the Gospels? Who is this divine Son of Man who comes down out of heaven? Do you see Christ clearly?

The Christian's Desire to See God Face to Face
by Richard Sibbes (1577–1635)
Do you yearn to see Christ face to face? Richard Sibbes fans the flame of the Christian's desire to see God from Psalm 27:4 in an extraordinary treatise on the subject of the beatific vision.

Vain Imaginations in the Worship of God
by Jonathan Edwards, Samuel Willard, Jonathan Dickinson, Joshua Moodey, and Nathan Stone

The Simplicity of Holy Worship
by John Wilson (1588–1667)
Jesus Christ was very clear in John 4:24 about true worship. Wilson explains what it means to make worship not only simple, but according to God's directives.

The Glory of Evangelical Worship
by John Owen (1616-1683)
John Owen's work on both worship and psalm singing shows theological precision and hearty biblical exposition. Edward Hutchins (annexed to this work) on psalmody is nothing less than extraordinary.

*A Christian's True
Spiritual Worship to Jesus Christ*
by Stephen Charnock (1628-1680)

Charnock tackles John 4:24 and shows how true worship is dictated by the Supreme Lawgiver, Jesus Christ. Annexed to this work is Jonathan Clapham's excellent treatise on singing psalms.

True Worship
and the Consequences of Idolatry
by John Knox (1505-1572)
If God alone determines the manner in which sinners approach him, is any other kind of worship acceptable to Him?

Gospel Worship, or, The Right Manner of Sanctifying the name of God in General, in Hearing the Word, Receiving the Lord's Supper, and Prayer
by Jeremiah Burroughs (1599-1646)
This classic work by Burroughs deals with the Regulative Principle: God alone determines the manner in which sinners approach him. This is a life-transforming and Christ-glorifying biblical work.

How to Serve God in Private and Public Worship
by John Jackson (1600-1648)
Does the Regulative Principle only apply to public worship and not private worship? John Jackson shows how God's word is to be applied in both private and public worship. (This book is not for the faint at heart!)

The Christian's Charge Never to Offend God in Worship
by John Forbes (1568-1634)
Does your church honor God in its public worship? Forbes explains 1 Timothy 3:13-16 to reformed churches that claim to uphold true worship, but may be missing the mark. An amazing and powerful work for today's contemporary church.